MAY   2003

Cowboys and Cookouts

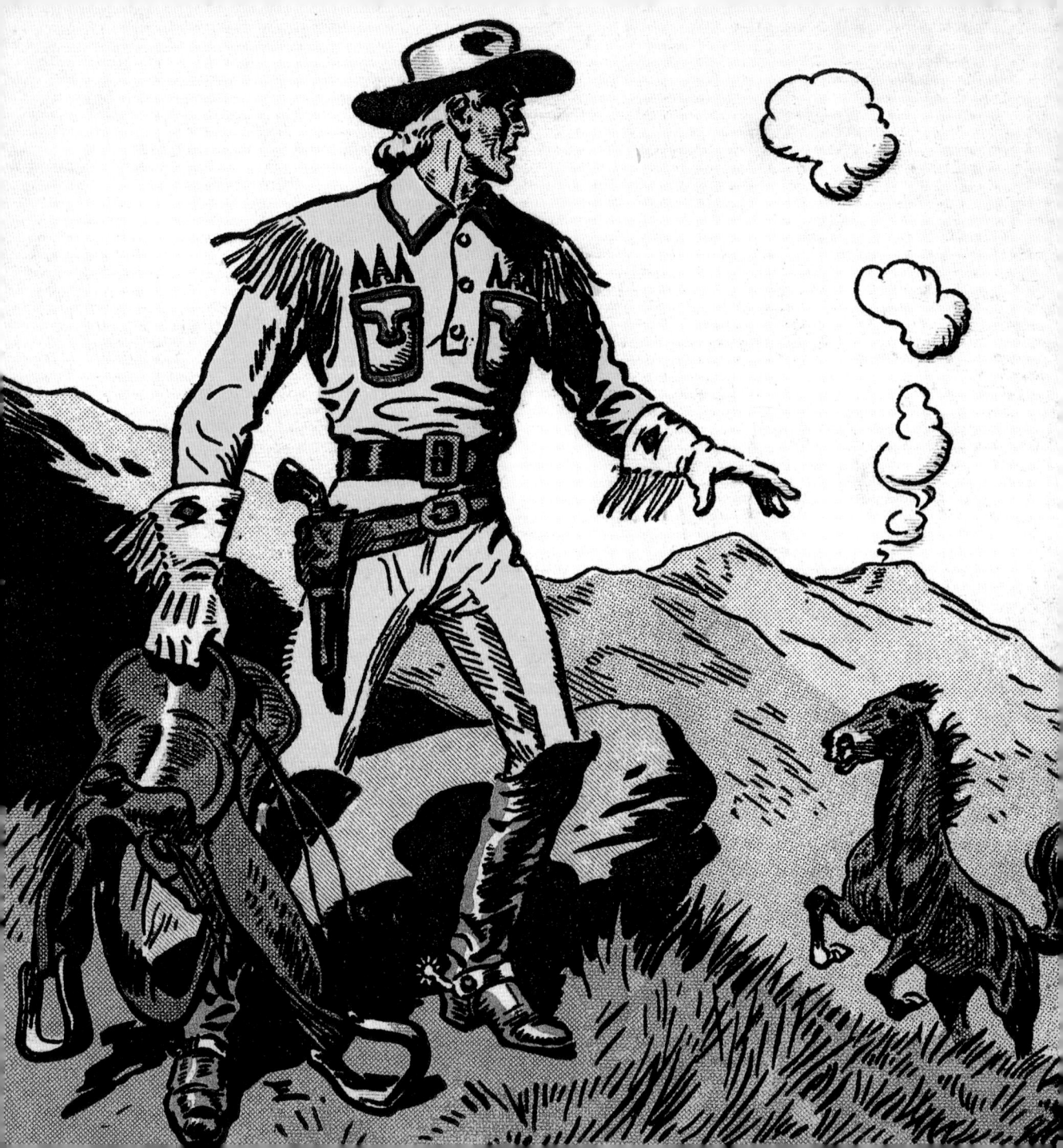

Cowboys and Cookouts

A TASTE OF THE OLD WEST

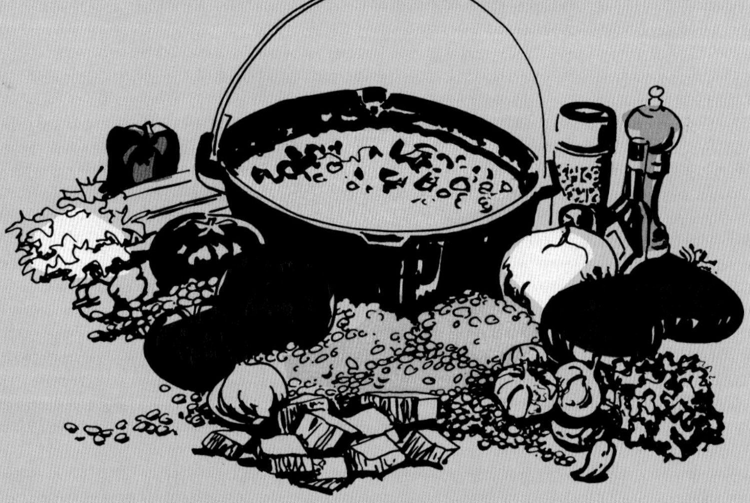

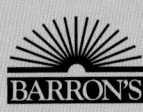

Lewis Esson

BARRON'S

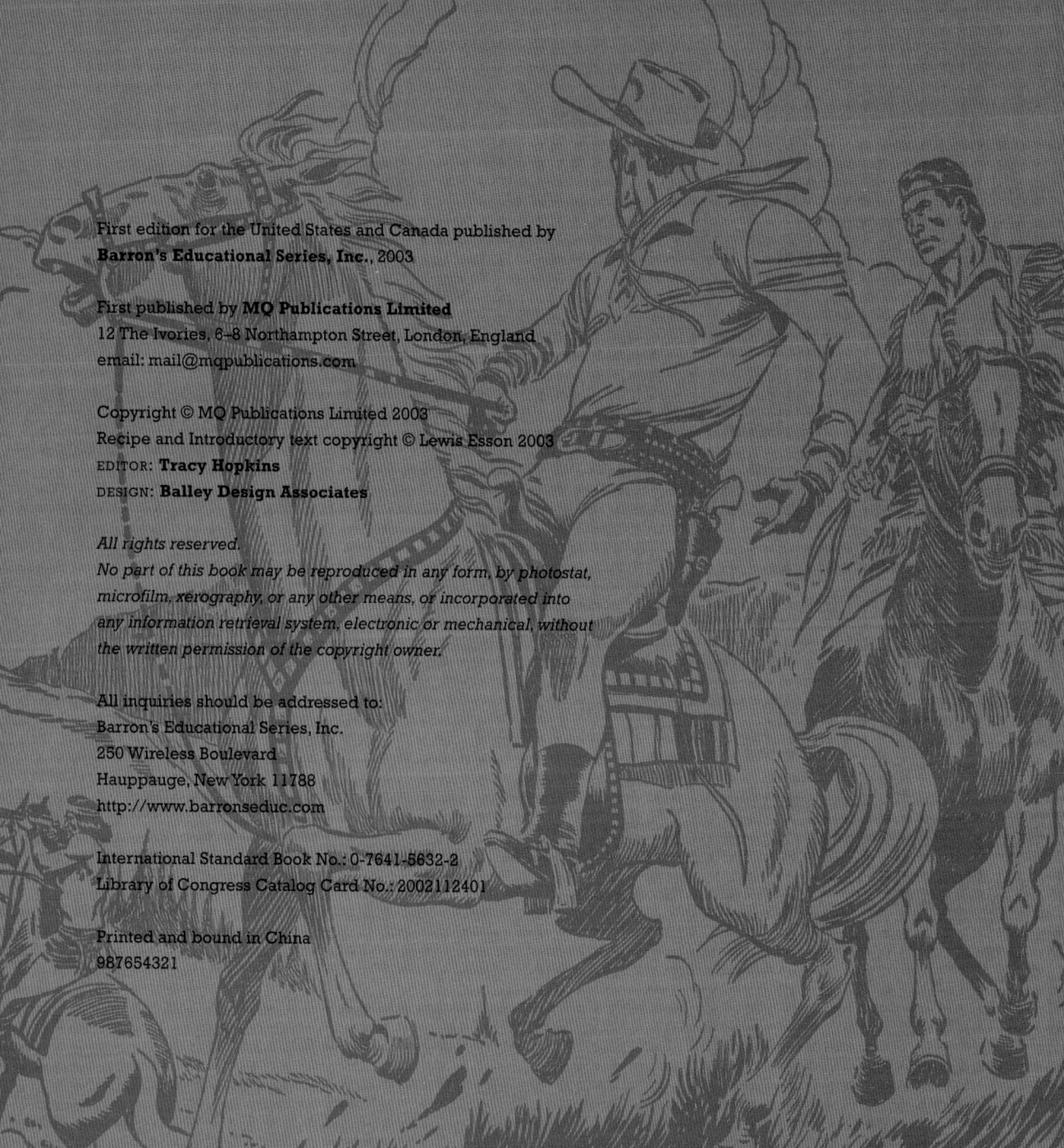

First edition for the United States and Canada published by
Barron's Educational Series, Inc., 2003

First published by **MQ Publications Limited**
12 The Ivories, 6–8 Northampton Street, London, England
email: mail@mqpublications.com

Copyright © MQ Publications Limited 2003
Recipe and Introductory text copyright © Lewis Esson 2003
EDITOR: **Tracy Hopkins**
DESIGN: **Balley Design Associates**

All inquiries should be addressed to:
Barron's Educational Series, Inc.
250 Wireless Boulevard
Hauppauge, New York 11788
http://www.barronseduc.com

International Standard Book No.: 0-7641-5632-2
Library of Congress Catalog Card No.: 2002112401

Printed and bound in China
987654321

CONTENTS

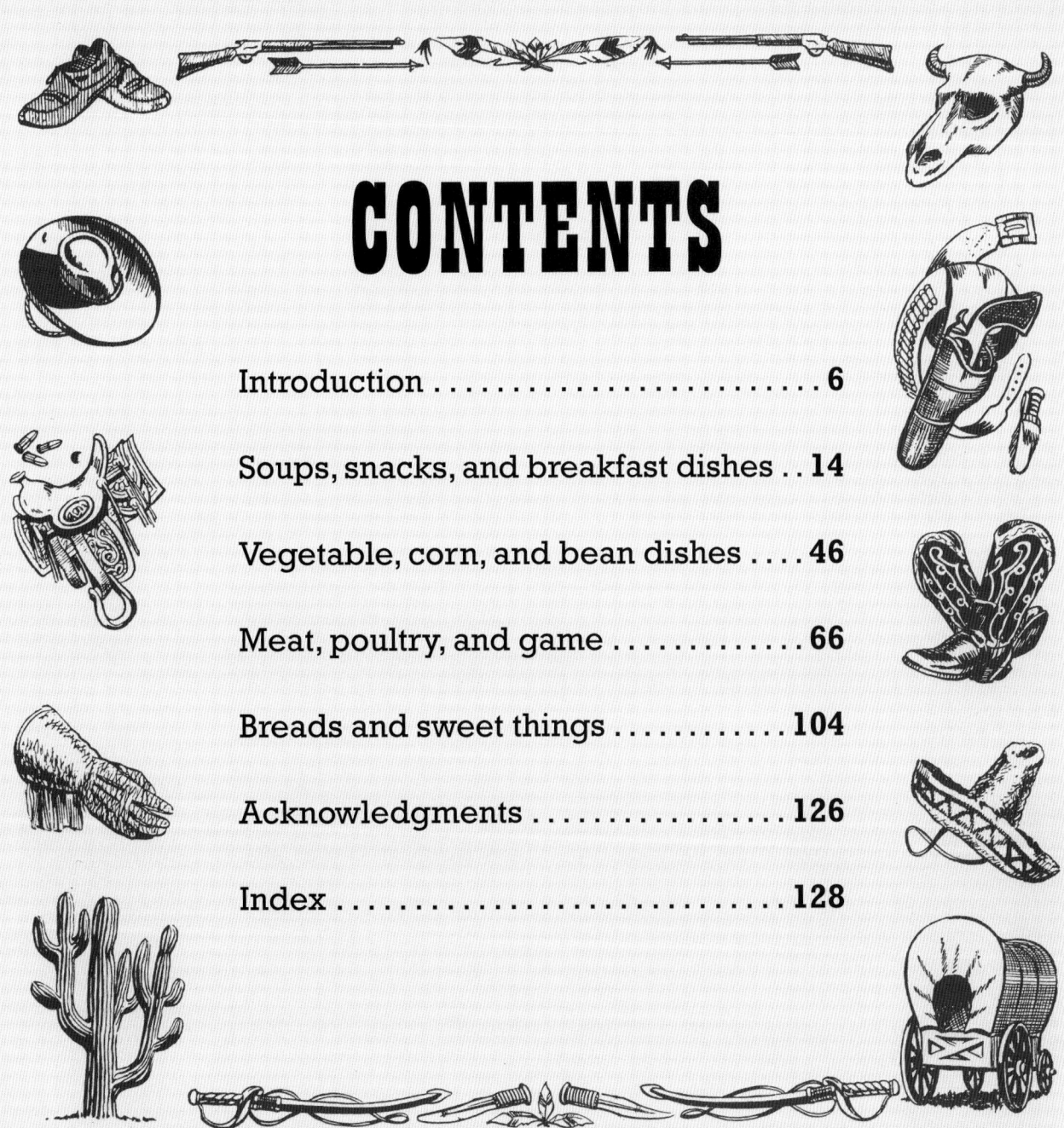

Introduction

It is a truly extraordinary phenomenon that a ragtag group of itinerant agricultural workers that really only flourished for a couple of decades in the latter half of the nineteenth century should have left such a lasting legacy. The cowboy era not only spawned its own entertainment form, in the rodeo and the activities of showmen like Buffalo Bill, but it also stimulated a wealth of extraordinary literature, inspired a mass of paintings and sculpture by artists as renowned as Frederic Remington, and eventually became a mainstay of the moving picture industry—further spreading its magic all over the world.

Even in its own time, the romance of the range and trail was recognized, and the native cowboys—including disaffected Texan Confederate soldiers, who couldn't find a place in the post-Civil War United States—were joined, from quite early on, by young bloods from all points of the compass, hoping to savor the unique and heady mix of danger and freedom that was cowboy life. Many British and Irish immigrants were to be found on the trail, and even members of the European aristocracy came to hunt buffalo or manage cattle ranches. For instance, the entrepreneurial French nobleman, the Marquis de Mores, has left a lasting legacy in Medora, North Dakota, where he became a rancher—and Theodore Roosevelt's neighbor—in 1883.

During the 1860s, 70s, and 80s, cattle ranches rapidly sprang up across the Great Plains, and cowboys were hired to drive the Texas Longhorn cattle for many miles across the prairies to railheads for onward shipment into the North and East. Several enterprising cattle ranchers and trail pioneers made huge profits because cattle could be worth far more in the North than in the Texas markets. The early cattle trails from Texas through the Indian Territory, such as the Sedalia Trail, were not an immediate success, but more routes soon followed and became well-established. The Chisholm Trail to the Abilene railhead in Kansas was the most famous, and the Western Trail to

Dodge City, Kansas, was also well-used—both Abilene and Dodge City grew rapidly into busy cattle towns, where the cowboys relaxed after their arduous months on the trail. Charles Goodnight and fellow rancher Oliver Loving established the Goodnight-Loving Trail that veered West into New Mexico and Colorado. Here they found new markets for their Texas cattle by supplying the mining towns, army camps, and even the Indian reservations. Despite the financial success of all these trails, they were fraught with countless dangers for the trailhands, including perilous weather and various physical hardships that they simply could not avoid.

The cowboys usually traveled the trails in crews of twelve, including their leader—the trail boss—and the cook. The latter, known variously as "cookie," "coosie," or "the old lady," also served as doctor, dentist, barber, banker, undertaker, referee, father confessor, and even mother. He drove and ran the "chuck wagon," which not only served as mobile kitchen but often carried all their supplies, including foodstuffs, medical supplies (if any), ammunition, and bedding. The chuck wagon was the only home the cowboys knew on a lonely cattle drive, and meal times were the highlight of their day. Among the basic items of cooking equipment stored in the wagon were an assortment of pots and pans (including the all-important coffee pot), skillets, and almost always a few Dutch ovens. This large cast-iron pot could be placed directly on the fire or hung over it, to allow subtle gradation of temperature within it. Tightly sealed and with the bottom and sides well-greased, it could function like an oven, allowing the "baking" of breads and biscuits, as well as being used for the making of the one-pot stews that were the mainstay of chuck wagon cuisine.

Throughout the book, my aim has been to give a flavor of the food enjoyed from the chuck wagon in the hope that you might use it to enrich your repertoire when preparing a "cookout" or just grilling in your back-yard. The cooking instructions are simple, so they can be applied across the board to open-fire cooking as well as to grilling.

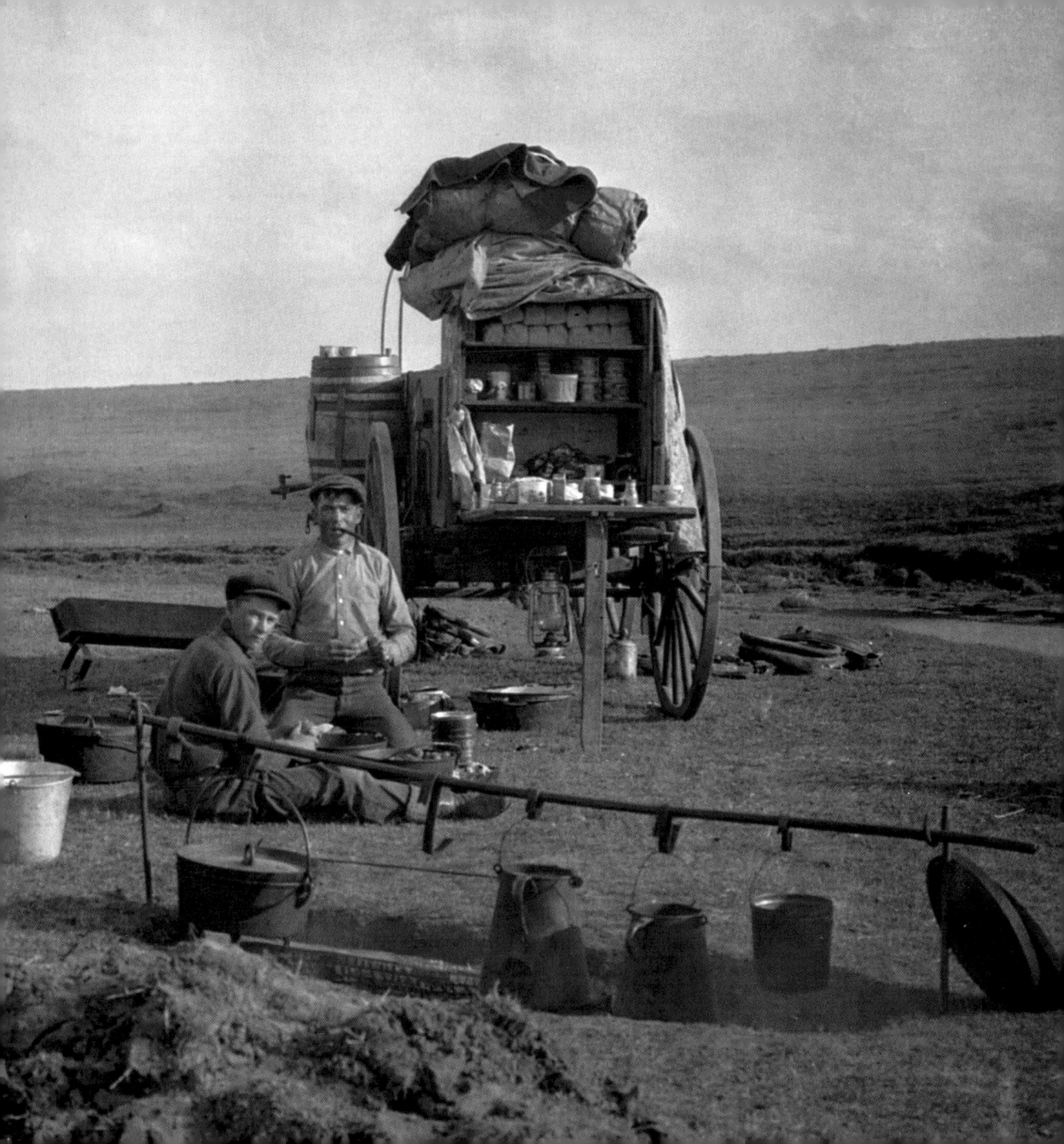

The Chuck Wagon

Cattleman Charles Goodnight claimed to have invented the prototype chuck wagon in 1866, but lots of ranchers and cowboys had been using homemade wagons as mobile kitchens for many years before Goodnight made his model. These specially converted wagons with their versatile chuck boxes or mess chests were crucial to the cowboys. The chuck wagon was their larder, their kitchen, and often their supply wagon, and without it the long cattle drives into the North would have been almost impossible. The chuck wagon was the center of the cowboys' working and social lives.

"The chuckwagon was a commissary on wheels, a stout wagon covered with canvas and equipped with a box at the rear for storing tin dishes, a Dutch oven, a frying pan, kettle, and coffee pot. The standard staples also had their exact places: green-berry coffee, salt pork, cornmeal, flour, and beans. For fresh meat, of course, there was always plenty of beef handy. A folding leg was usually attached to the chuckbox lid, so that it formed a table when lowered for action."

FROM THE AMERICAN WEST by Dee Brown

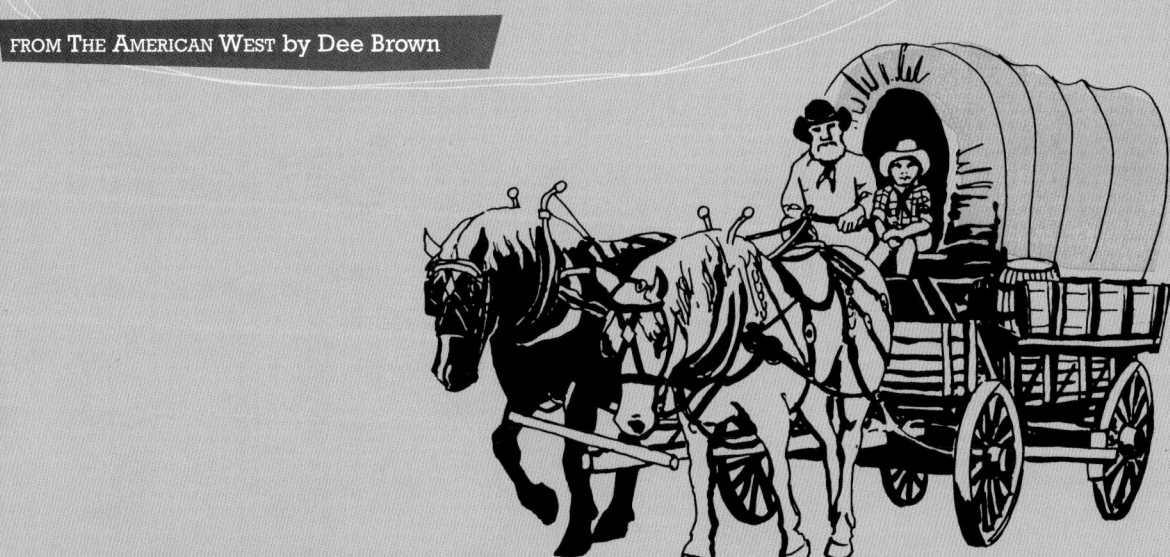

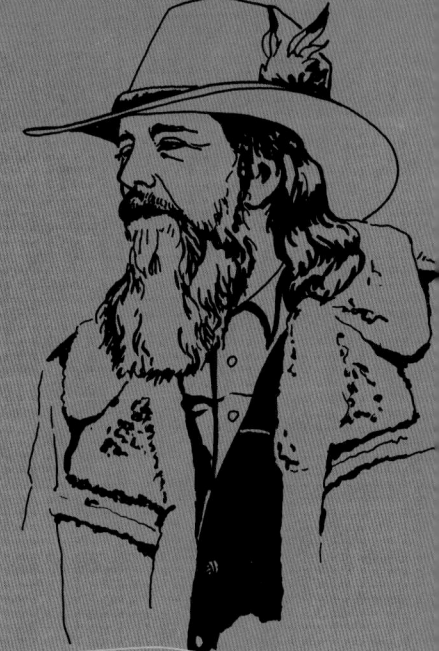

Cookie

The cook was the "Old Lady" of the trail drive, and he kept the home fires burning out on the range. He was paid twice as much as the cowboys, but he was also the first man up and the last man to bed—and was one of the most indispensable members of the team. He had many nicknames, including cookie, coosie (from the Spanish word for cook, *cocinero*), biscuit shooter, bean burner, old pud, belly cheater, gut robber, dough puncher, greasy belly, and sourdough. His assistant, who gathered the firewood, peeled the potatoes, and did all the cooking chores, was called the hoodlum.

This is what Theodore Roosevelt had to say about the cooks he met at the roundups at the Little Missouri in 1883:

"As soon as I reached the meeting-place I would find out the wagon to which I was assigned. Riding to it, I turned my horses into the saddle-band and reported to the wagon boss, or, in his absence, to the cook—always a privileged character, who was allowed and expected to order men around. He would usually grumble savagely and profanely about my having been put with his wagon, but this was merely conventional on his part; and if I sat down and said nothing he would probably soon ask me if I wanted anything to eat, to which the correct answer was that I was not hungry and would wait until meal-time."

Theodore Roosevelt, 1913, FROM AN AUTOBIOGRAPHY; "IV: IN COWBOY LAND"

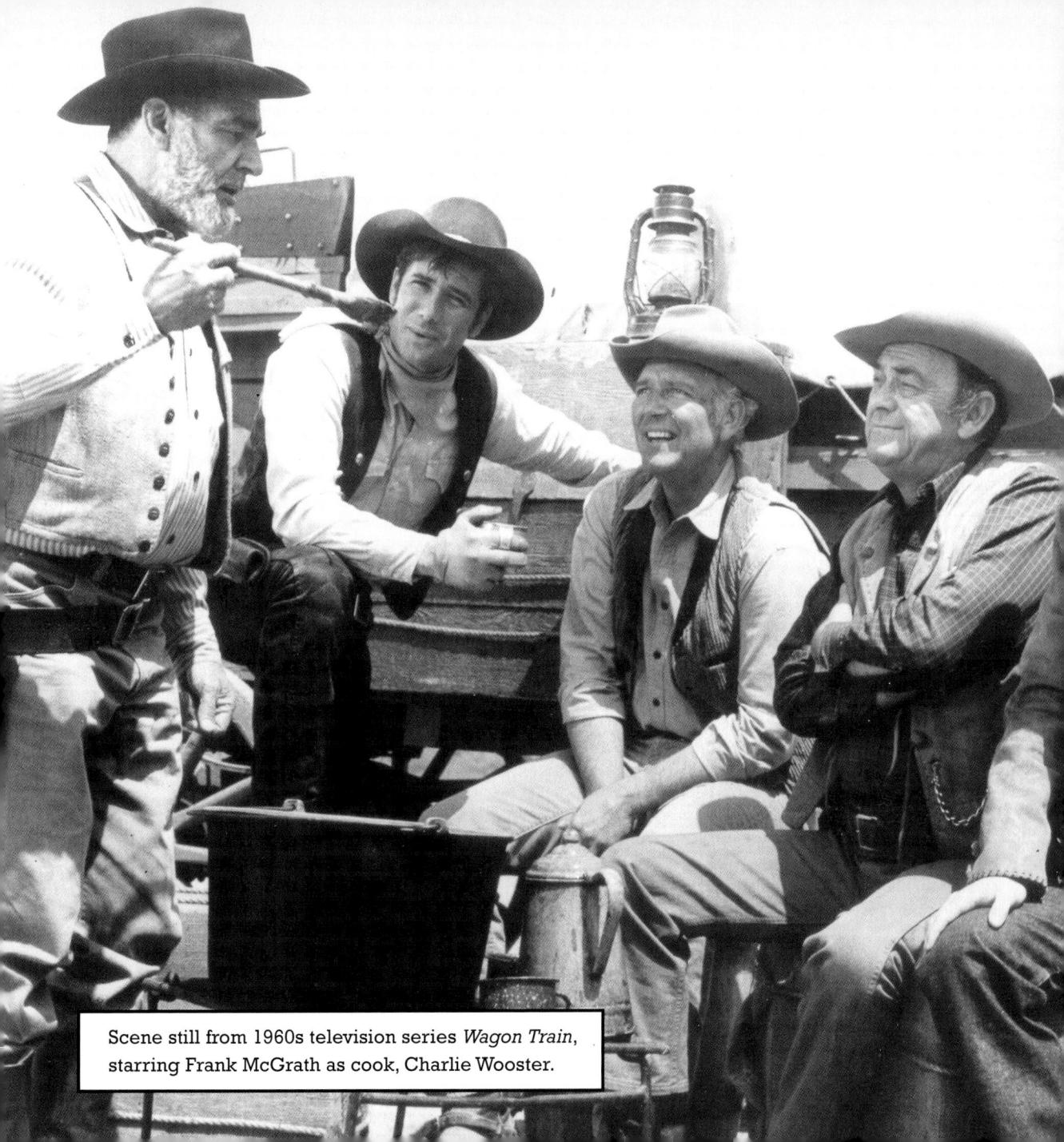

Scene still from 1960s television series *Wagon Train*, starring Frank McGrath as cook, Charlie Wooster.

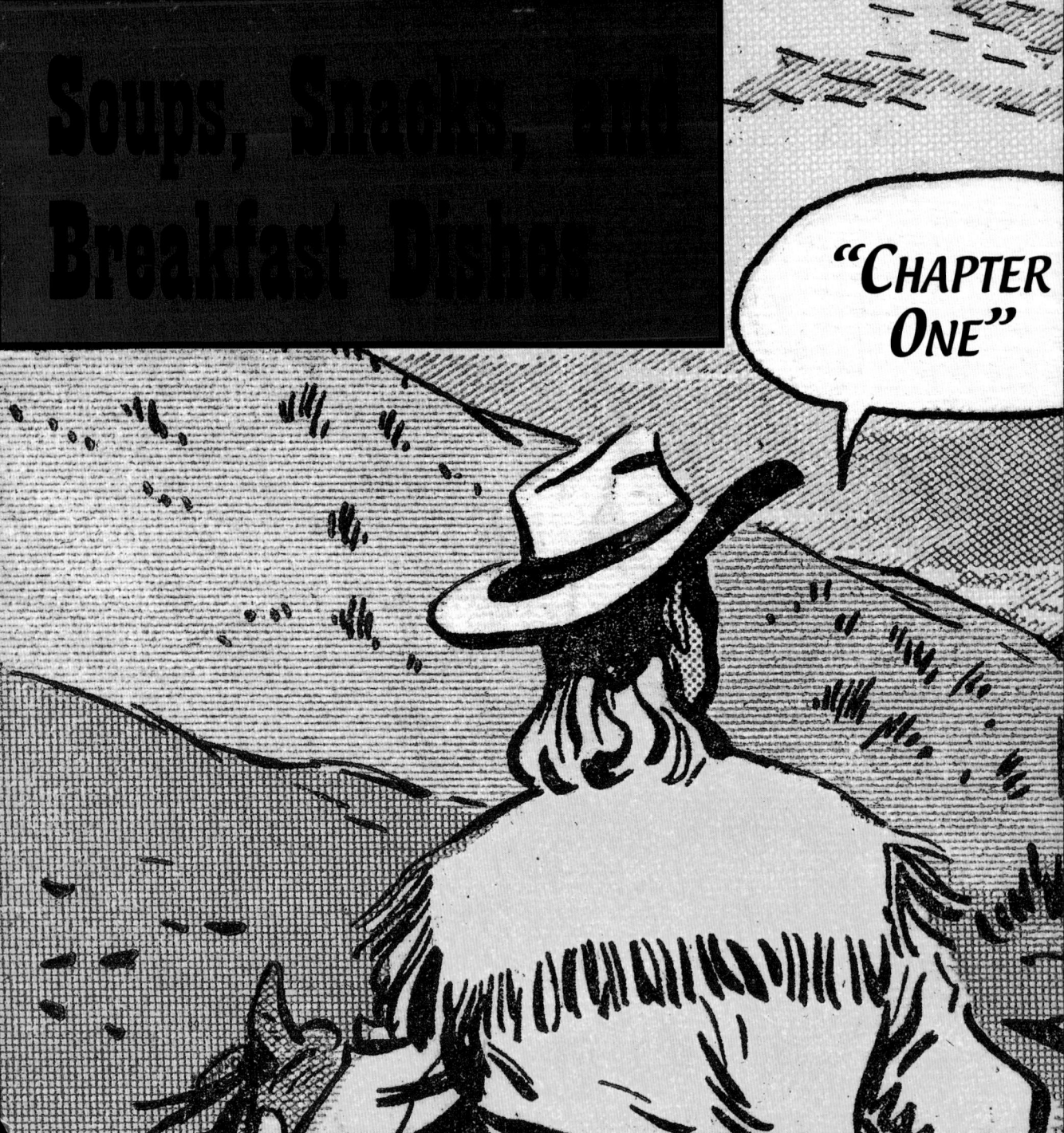

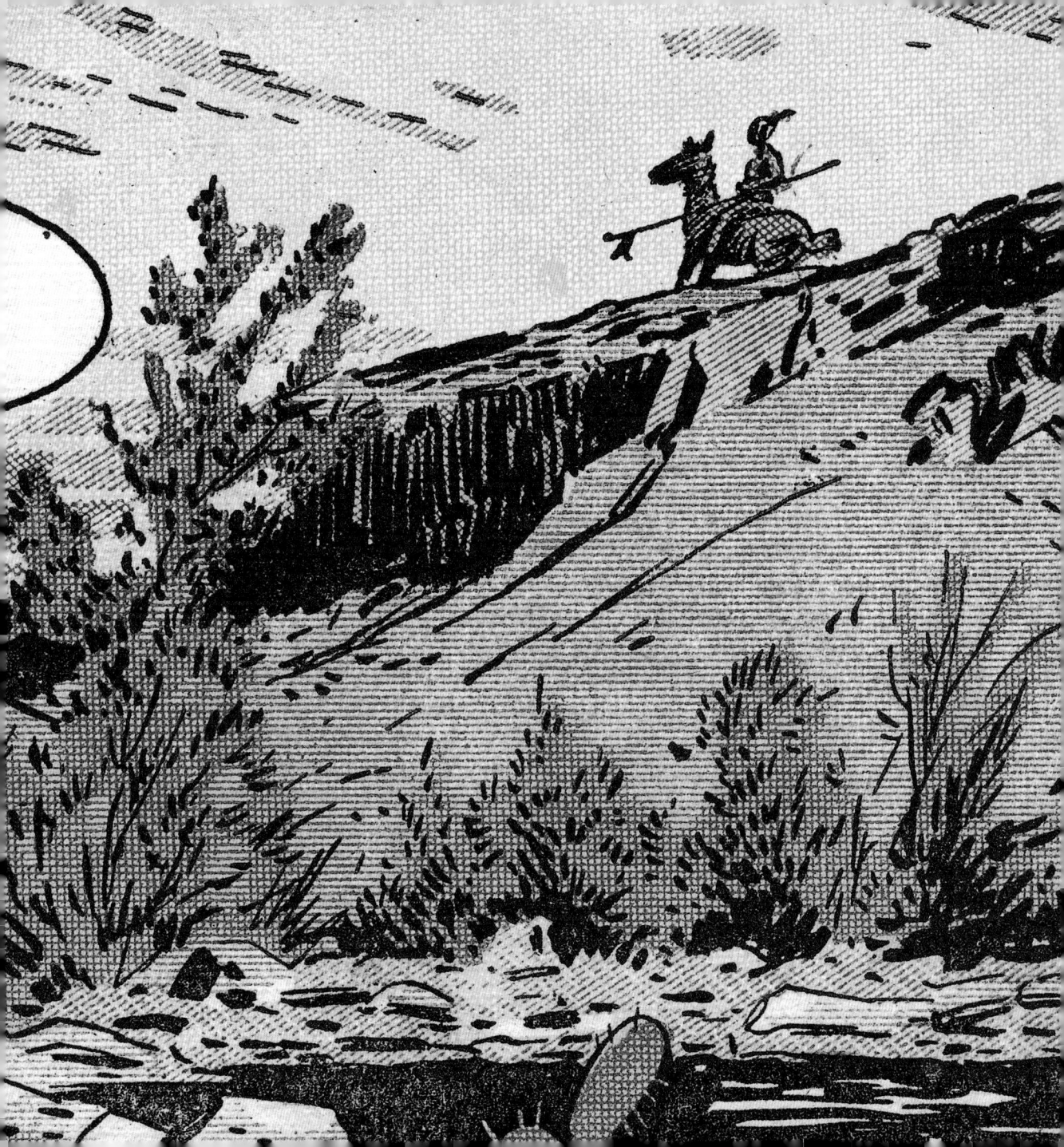

*B*reakfast was a pretty important event for the cowboy as there would almost certainly be no other cooked meal until dinner at the end of the day. Cookie would normally be up several hours before the other men, getting this meal together. He would probably have done quite a lot of the preparation, like peeling potatoes and preparing his sourdough starter, the night before.

Cookie would get the men up well before dawn so they could be out on the range before first light. He would serve them their coffee and a fairly substantial meal, and then pass out packs of cold biscuits, pieces of cooked ham or bacon and, possibly, a pickle or two to sustain them through the long day. If they were camped near a farm or town, fresh milk or eggs might be available. Eggs were considered a rare treat (cookie normally kept them for sweet dishes), and they were often scrambled with jerky. Bacon was popular for breakfast as it kept well, was easy to cook, supplied extras for snacks, and provided cookie with drippings for the evening meal.

Soups or soupy stews were often served as part of the evening meal as a means both of warming the men and of making something substantial and nourishing out of little more than bones, beans, and leftovers.

Sour Milk Pancakes with Bacon

Serves 4 (makes about 12 pancakes)

10 oz./scant 2 cups (275 g) flour
2 tsp. sugar
1½ tsp. baking powder
1 tsp salt
1 pint/2 cups (450 ml) buttermilk

1 oz./2 tbsp. (25 g) butter, melted
2 eggs, well beaten
fried bacon and maple syrup
(optional), to serve

1 Sift the flour, sugar, baking powder, and salt together into a mixing bowl. Stir in the buttermilk and add the melted butter. Stir in the beaten eggs lightly with a few strokes to make a batter.

2 Heat a dry frying pan or griddle until quite hot (a drop of water bounces from it and sputters) and drop heaping spoonfuls of the batter onto it. Turn the pancakes over when bubbles appear on the uncooked surface and cook until golden brown on both sides.

3 Serve with fried bacon and maple syrup if you like.

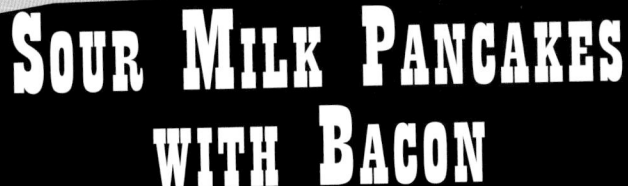

Mornin' Business

by Lee Henry

Rattlin' of pans in the pre-dawn light
Signals the end of a cold bitter night.

Jawin' and gratin' of the coffee grinders song
Says get up cowboy it's near breakin' dawn.

A grouchy ole figure with pot hook in hand
Reflects a lifetime of cookin' with his wrinkles and tan.

His breakfast from memory is simple to fix
It's salt pork, coffee, sour dough and lick.

His kitchen of canvas, chuckwagon and Hanes
Prances and dances in the flickering flames.

From inside the chuckbox the Cookie removes
A large sack of flour and a bottle of booze.

With his back to the bedrolls from the bottle he takes
A nip of "White Lightnin'" to ward off the snakes.

The tools of his trade, a bowl he has kept
Thru thunder and lightnin' and rustlers he 's met.

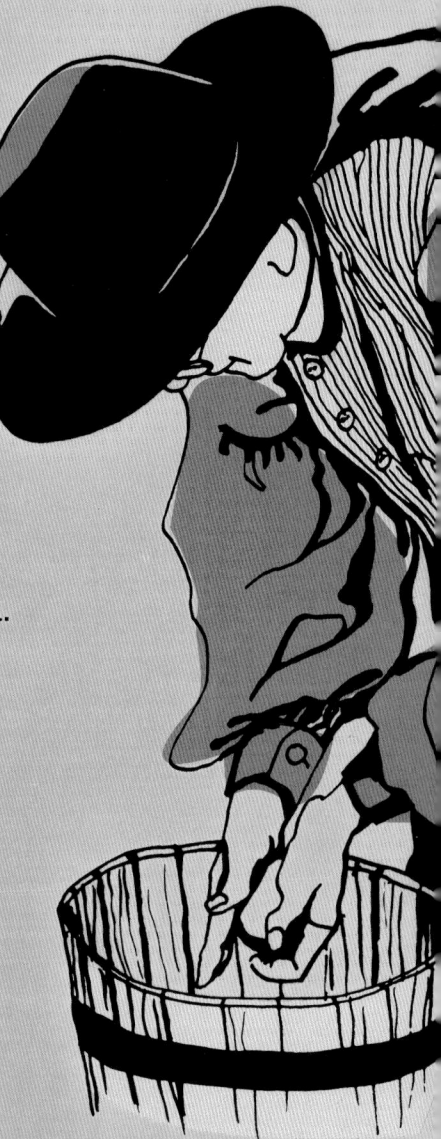

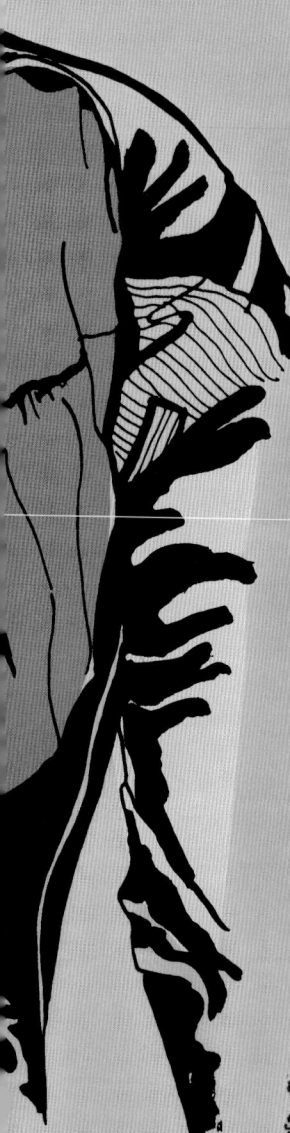

Washed in streams and scrubbed by the sands
His large wooden bowl he carved with his hands.

Blendin' the lard in the fixins' so neat
From the crock pours the sourdough, it's sour but sweet.

The biscuits are cut and then to the Dutch
Are crowded together by the master's touch.

The coals from the fire on the lid with a lip
Are hot as a Colt drawn from the hip.

The golden brown sourdoughs from his Dutch oven pan
Has filled the craw of many-a-man.

With his back to the cowboys ridin', over the crest
A nip he will take before attackin' the mess.

With bottle in hand, and the marks from a quirt
As he Toasts, "Thanks Cookie" Cut in the Dirt.

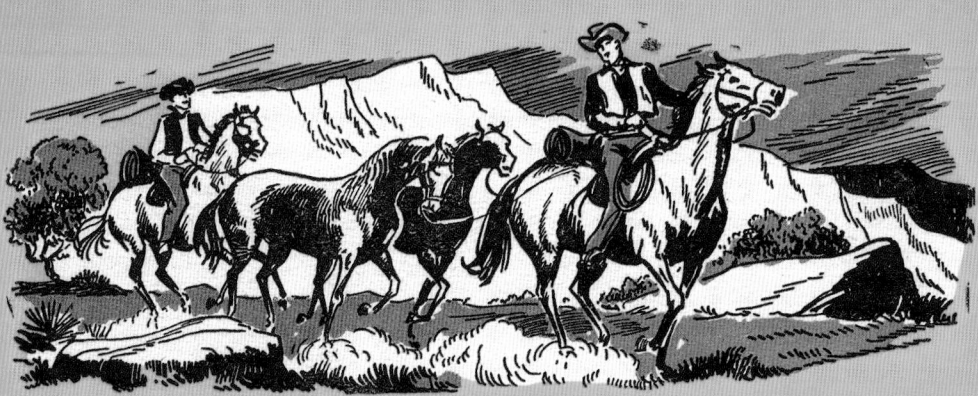

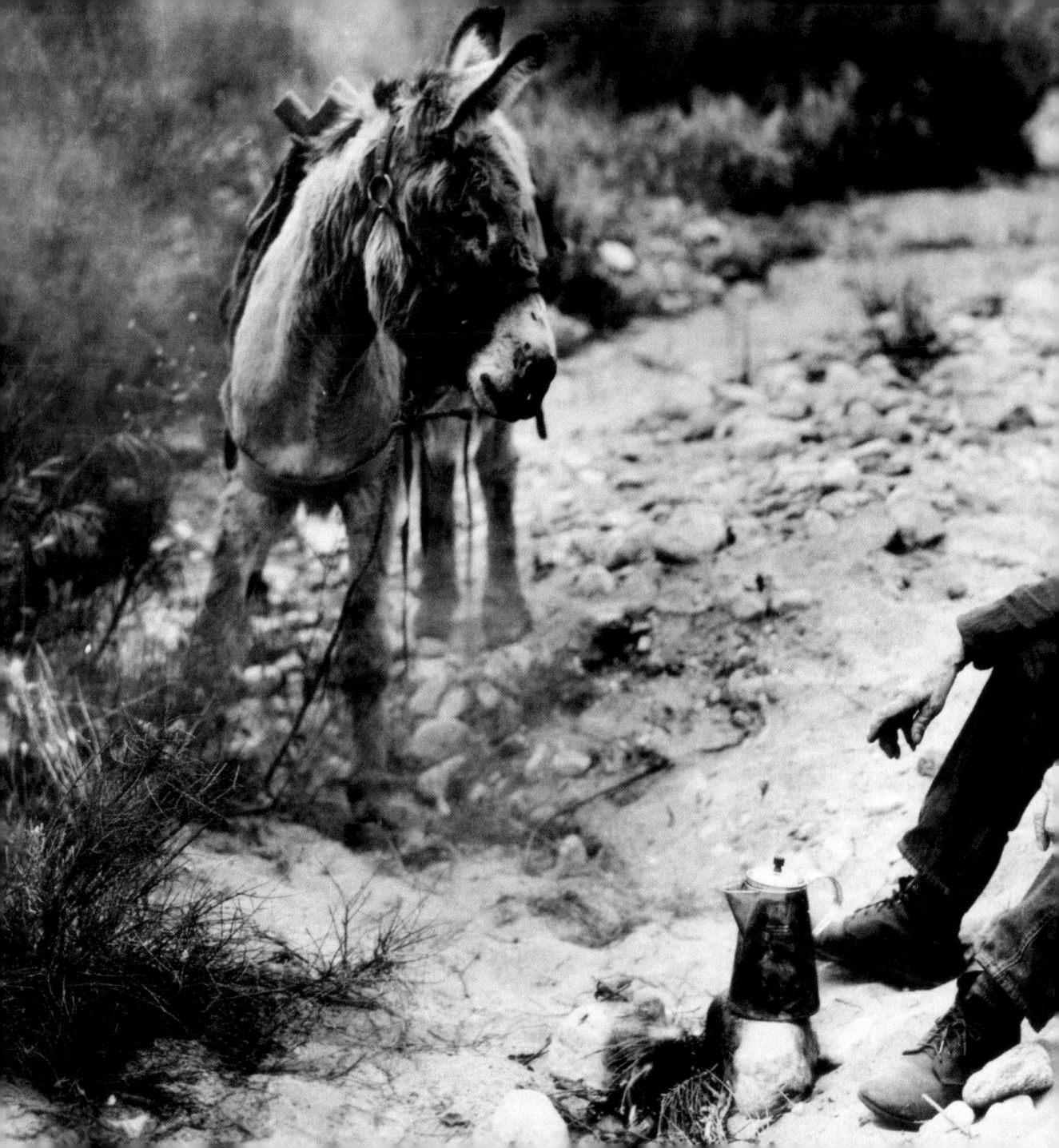

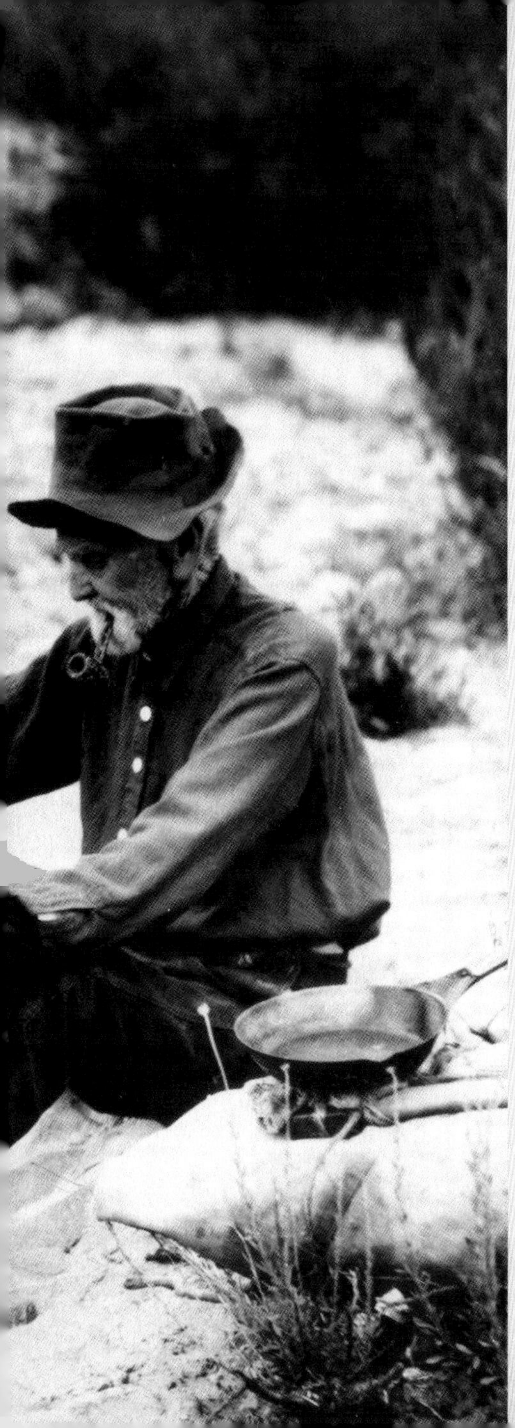

"ALL AMERICA LIES AT THE END OF THE WILDERNESS ROAD, AND OUR PAST IS NOT A DEAD PAST, BUT STILL LIVES ON IN US. OUR FOREFATHERS HAD CIVILIZATION INSIDE THEMSELVES, THE WILD OUTSIDE. WE LIVE IN THE CIVILIZATION THEY CREATED, BUT WITHIN US THE WILDERNESS STILL LINGERS. WHAT THEY DREAMED, WE LIVE, AND WHAT THEY LIVED, WE DREAM."

T. K. Whipple
FROM STUDY OUT THE LAND

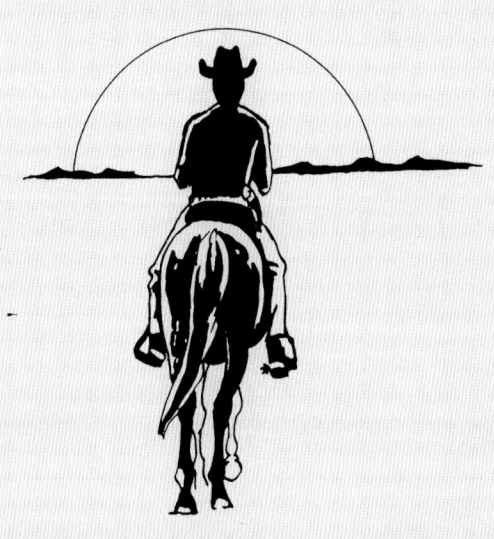

SOURDOUGH HOTCAKES

1½ cups (350 ml) evaporated milk
8 fl. oz./1 cup (225 ml) lukewarm water
1½ oz./3 tbsp. (45 g) sugar
12 oz./1½ cups (350 g) flour
½ tsp. salt
½ tsp. baking powder

For the sourdough starter:
¼ oz. (7.5 g) active dry yeast
8 fl. oz./1 cup (225 ml) warm water
½ oz./3 tbsp. (15 g) sugar
6 oz./¾ cup (150 g) flour

1 The morning before, make the starter: In a large mixing bowl, dissolve the yeast in the warm water and let sit for 2 to 3 minutes. Then stir in the sugar. Sift in the flour and mix well. Cover and let sit in a warm place for 12 hours, stirring occasionally when you can.

2 That evening, in another large mixing bowl, mix one-third of this starter with the evaporated milk, lukewarm water, sugar, and flour to make a batter. Cover and let sit overnight at room temperature. (Feed the starter with another 2½ oz./5 tbsp. (75 g) flour, 4 fl. oz./½ cup (125 ml) water, and 1 tsp. sugar, mix well, and keep in the refrigerator until needed again for the next batch.)

3 The next morning, stir the salt and baking powder into the now creamy and bubbly batter.

4 Heat a dry frying pan or griddle until quite hot (a drop of water bounces from it and sputters) and drop the batter onto it, about 1 cup at a time. Turn the hotcakes over when bubbles appear on the uncooked surface and cook until golden brown on both sides.

If you are lucky enough to have any ripe berries on hand, they will go well with these hotcakes, either cooked in the batter or served with them.

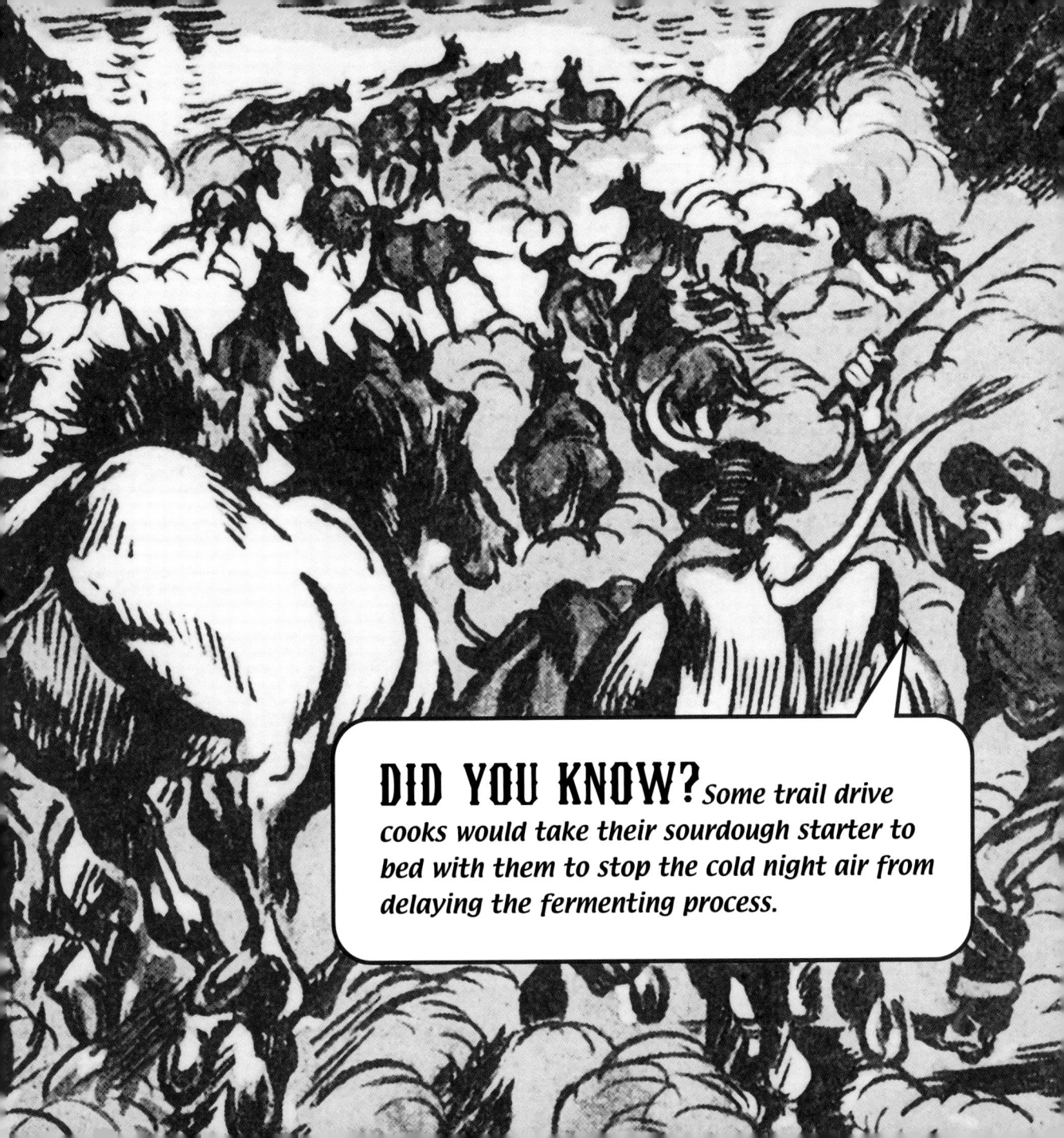

DID YOU KNOW? *Some trail drive cooks would take their sourdough starter to bed with them to stop the cold night air from delaying the fermenting process.*

BISCUITS ON STICKS

Makes about 18

1 lb./4 cups (450 g) flour
1½ tbsp. baking powder
1 tsp. salt

6 oz./¾ cup (175 g) cold lard
about 8 fl. oz./1 cup (225 ml)
cold milk

1 Combine the flour, baking powder, and salt in a large mixing bowl. Grate the lard into the bowl and mix in lightly with the fingertips until the mixture resembles coarse crumbs.

2 Make a well in the center and pour in three-quarters of the milk. Sir until the dough starts to come away from the sides of the bowl. If too dry, add a little more milk a little at a time.

3 When smooth and pliable, turn the dough out on a lightly floured surface and knead quickly for a minute or so, folding no more than 10 times.

4 Divide the dough into about 18 pieces and flatten each out with your hands. Wrap each piece around the tip of a well-scrubbed, thick, green, nontoxic shrub branch that is long enough to use safely on the fire.

5 Cook over the fire or barbecue for about 10 minutes, turning from time to time, until golden brown all over.

6 When cool enough to handle, pull out the branch and fill the center of the biscuit with butter, cheese, jam, or even shredded meat and gravy.

You can flavor the biscuit dough by adding chili and/or grated cheese, chopped scallions, or cinnamon and sugar for a sweet taste.

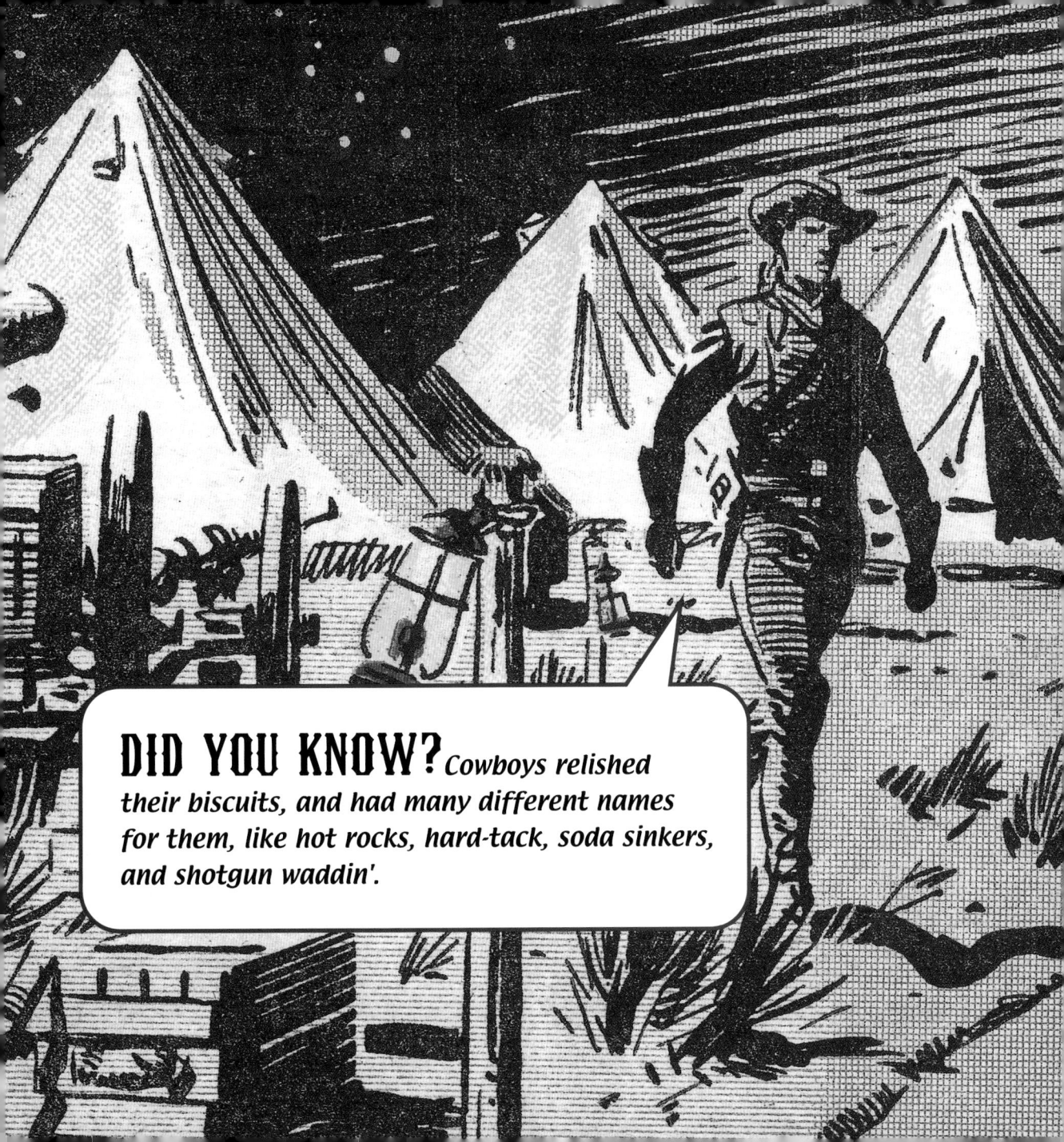

DID YOU KNOW? *Cowboys relished their biscuits, and had many different names for them, like hot rocks, hard-tack, soda sinkers, and shotgun waddin'.*

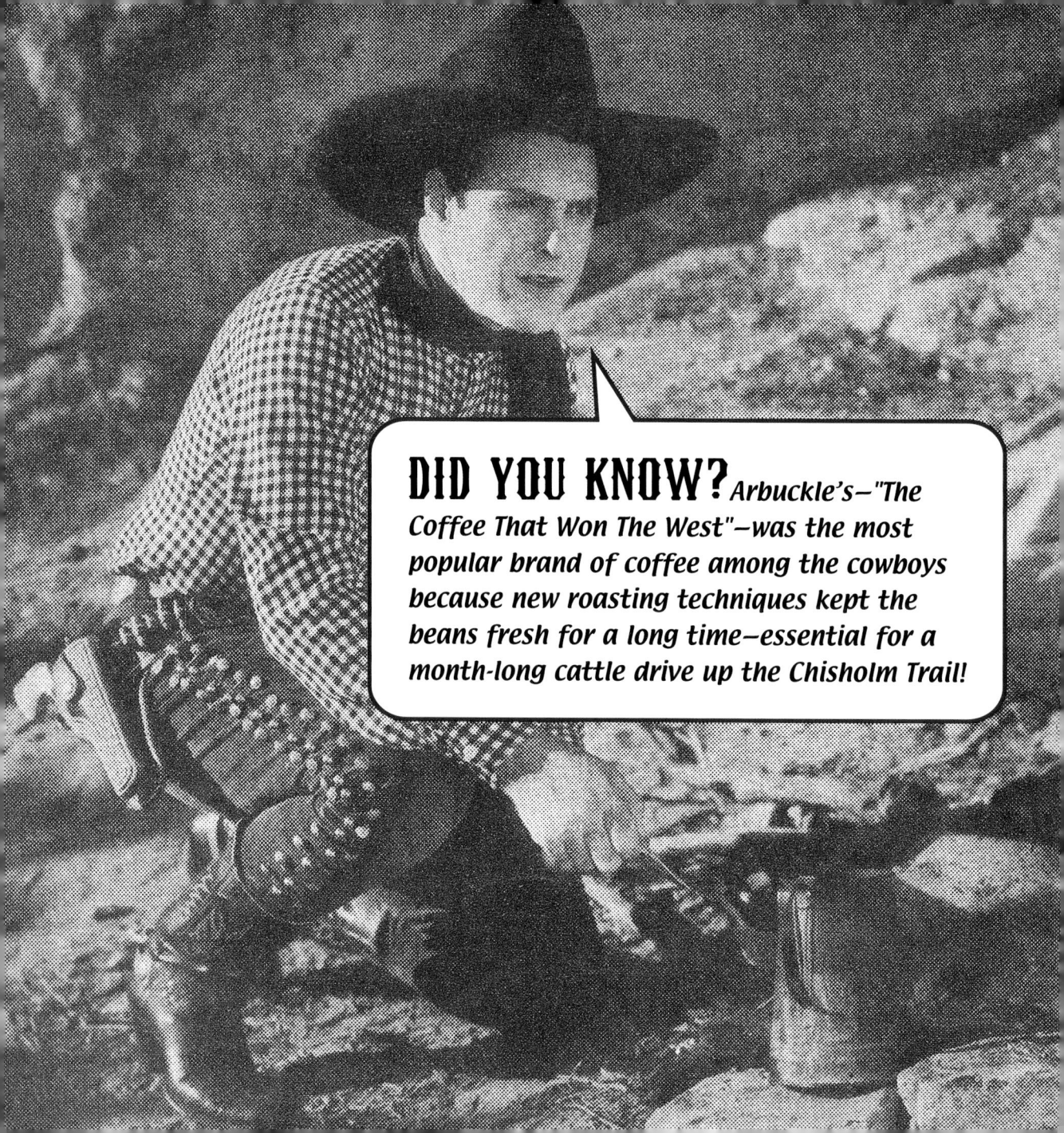

COFFEE, COWBOY-STYLE

Makes 8 cups

Cowboys insisted on actually cooking the grounds to make good coffee, and the eggshell (some actually included the whole egg) helps to keep it from becoming bitter. Adding cold water before pouring settles the grounds.

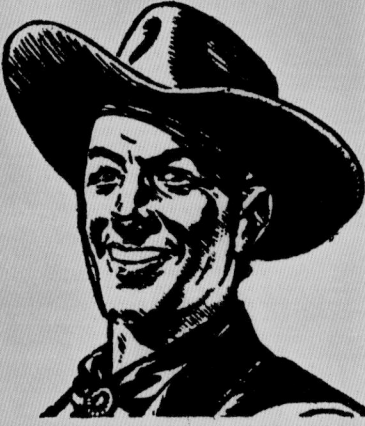

**3½ oz./7 tbsp. (100 g) ground roast coffee
crushed shell of 1 egg**

1 Bring 8 cups/2 liters of water to a boil.

2 Put the coffee and eggshell in a bag and work to mix well. If you are grinding your own beans, add the eggshell at the end and pulse to mix.

3 Put the coffee and eggshell mixture into a coffee pot and pour in the boiling water. Simmer for 4 minutes, add a half-cup of cold water and serve.

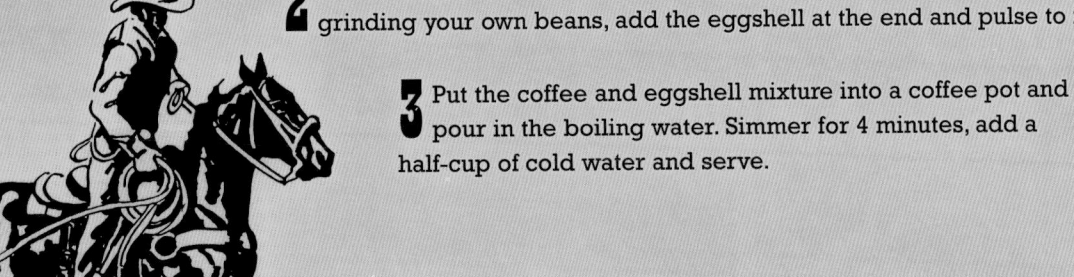

Cowboy Coffee

by Rod Miller

Just boil some river water
And a big handful of grounds,
Both of which you add to
As the level in the pot goes down.

If you want some extra body
Throw in some used horseshoes,
And now and then to rich it up
Add a pinch of snoose.

That's how real cowboys like their coffee,
And they can't seem to get enough.
Maybe that's why I ain't much of a hand—
I never touch the stuff.

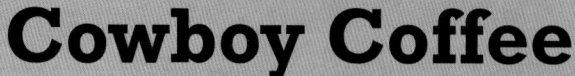
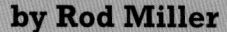

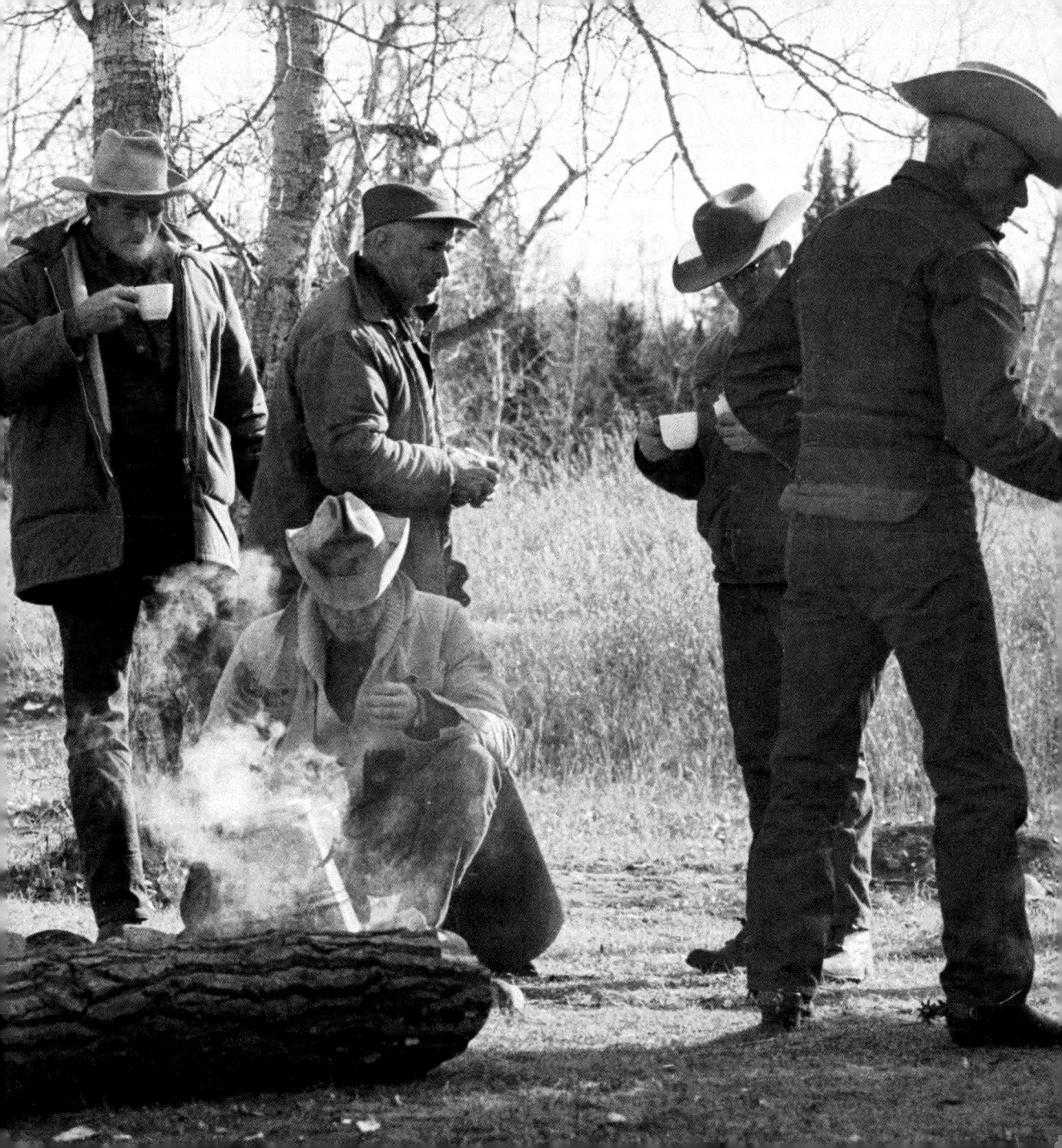

SWEET POTATO HASH BROWNS

Serves 6

3 tbsp. oil
1 onion, sliced
salt and pepper
4–6 sweet potatoes, peeled and
diced into ¾-in. (2-cm) pieces

1 small red or green pepper, deseeded
and cut into ½-in. (1-cm) pieces

1 Heat the oil in a large heavy-duty frying pan and cook the onions with some salt and pepper to taste until softened.

2 Add the sweet potatoes with some more seasoning and cook, stirring frequently until golden, about 15 minutes.

3 Add the chopped pepper and continue cooking, stirring regularly until nicely browned and everything is tender, about 20 minutes more.

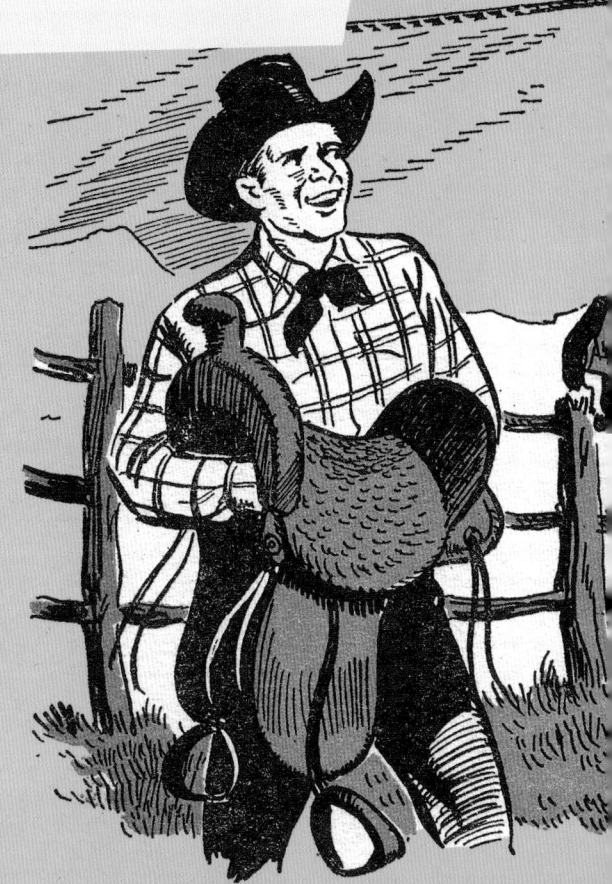

ROUNDUP POTATOES AND EGGS

Serves 4

1 oz./2 tbsp. (25 g) butter
2 tbsp. oil
1¼ lb. (575 g) potatoes, diced
1 onion, finely chopped

8 large eggs
salt and pepper
good dash of Tabasco sauce

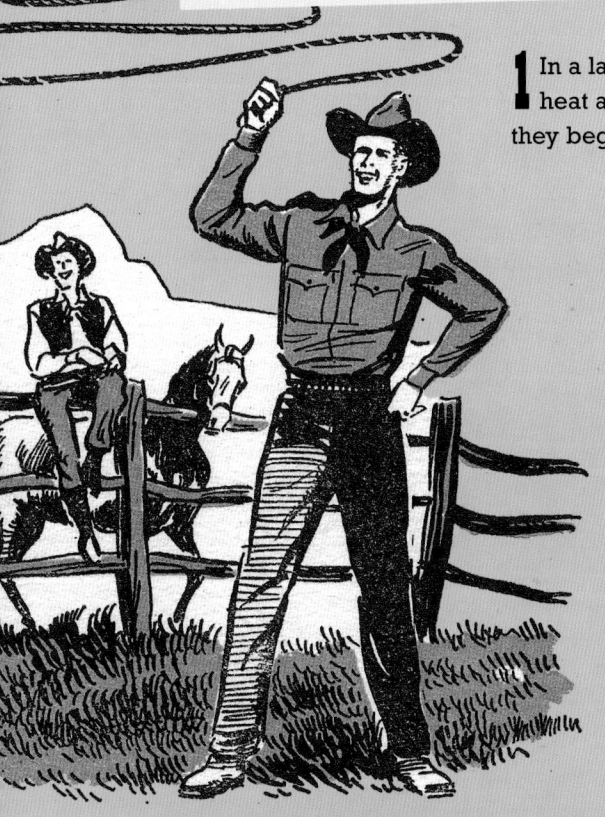

1 In a large frying pan, heat the butter and oil over medium heat and fry the potatoes, stirring from time to time until they begin to brown and soften.

2 Add the onion and cook for about 10 minutes, stirring frequently, until the potatoes are tender and well browned (possibly increasing the heat slightly toward the end of this time).

3 Beat the eggs together in a bowl, seasoning them to taste with salt, pepper, and Tabasco, and pour into the potatoes. Stir constantly for about 5 minutes, until the eggs are just set but still slightly soft.

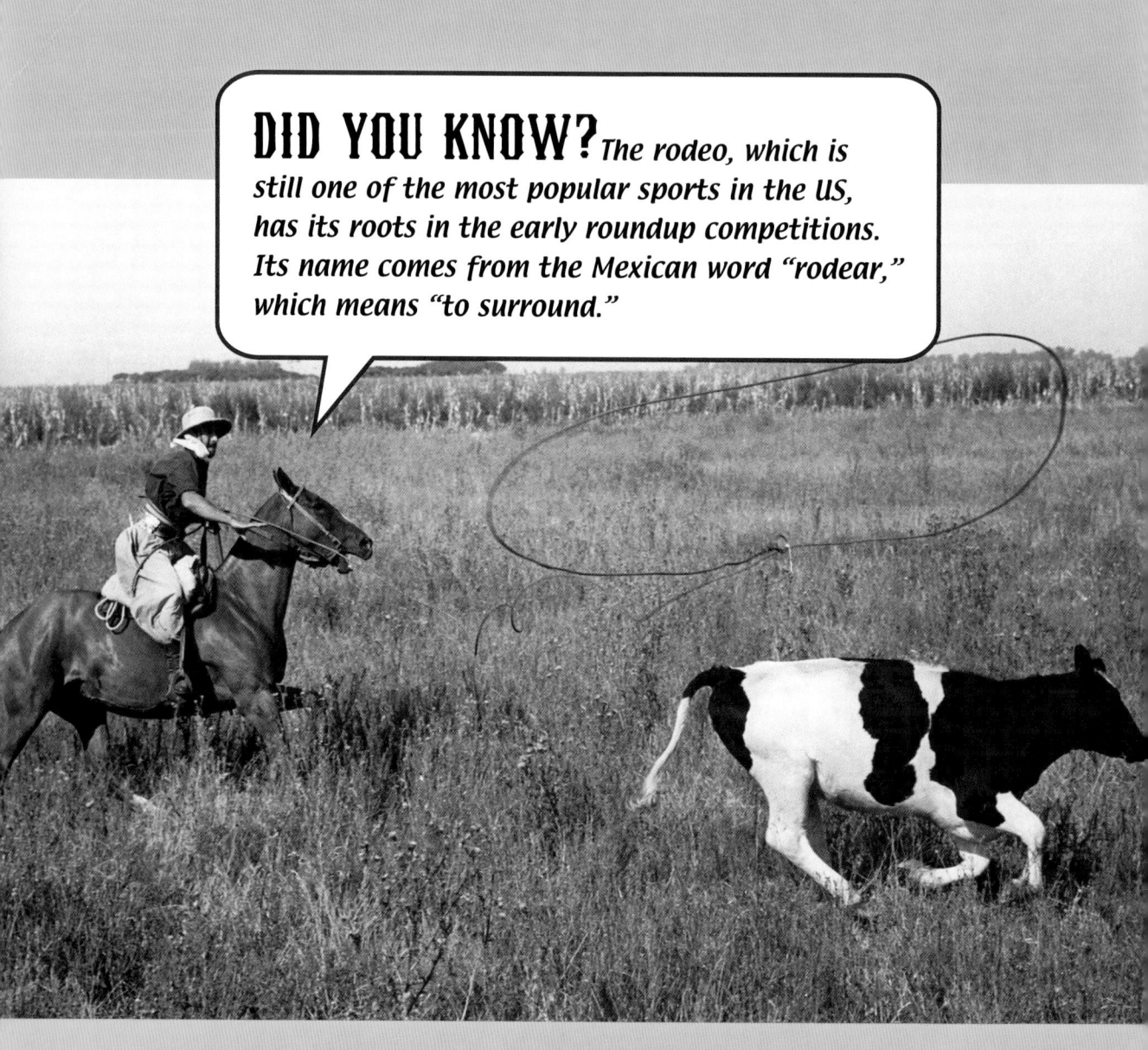

DID YOU KNOW? *The rodeo, which is still one of the most popular sports in the US, has its roots in the early roundup competitions. Its name comes from the Mexican word "rodear," which means "to surround."*

The Roundup

Before the cowhands could start out on an arduous cattle trail, the cattle had to be gathered and branded. These roundups required all of a cowboy's riding and roping skills, not to mention courage and determination! Roundups were necessary throughout the year for the branding of new calves and to separate the different ranches' herds. The same roping and cutting skills were also used to round up strays on the trail. The cowboys loved to show off their prowess at these roundups, and rivalries and unofficial competitions quickly began to spring up across the West.

"In those days on a cow ranch the men were apt to be away on the various round-ups at least half the time. It was interesting and exciting work, and except for the lack of sleep on the spring and summer round-ups it was not exhausting work; compared to lumbering or mining or blacksmithing, to sit in the saddle is an easy form of labor. …"

"The spring and early summer round-ups were especially for the branding of calves. There was much hard work and some risk on a round-up, but also much fun. The meeting-place was appointed weeks beforehand, and all the ranchmen of the territory to be covered by the round-up sent their representatives. There were no fences in the West that I knew, and their place was taken by the cowboy and the branding-iron. The cattle wandered free. Each calf was branded with the brand of the cow it was following."

Theodore Roosevelt, 1913, FROM AN AUTOBIOGRAPHY; "IV: IN COWBOY LAND"

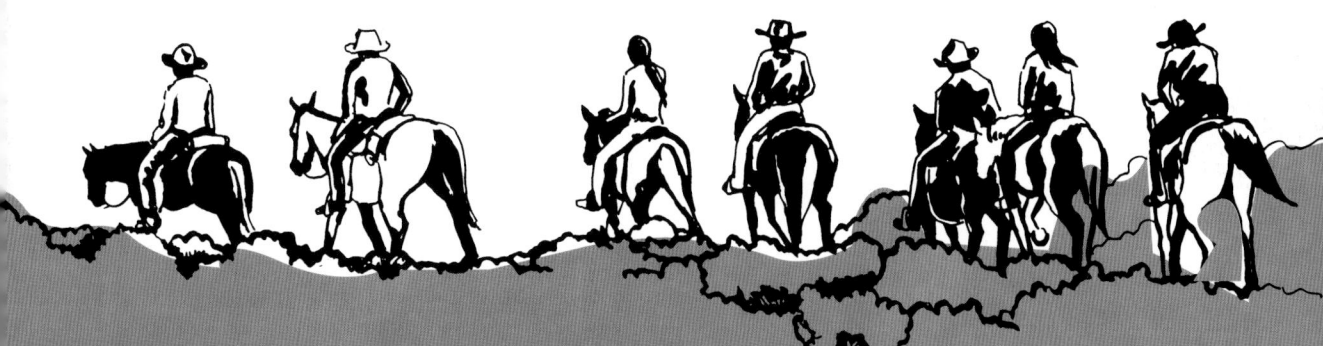

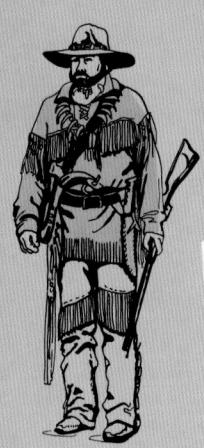

BREAKFAST TORTILLAS

Serves 4–6

6 small, dry, corn tortillas
oil, for deep-frying
1 onion, finely chopped
8 oz. (225 g) leftover cooked beef,
pork, or ham, cut into
bite-sized pieces

6 oz./¾ cup (150 g) mild cheddar
cheese, shredded

1 Chop or tear the tortillas into bite-sized pieces. Heat about 2 inches of oil in a
frying pan over medium to high heat until a piece of tortilla dropped in the oil
turns golden and crisp in a few seconds. Fry the pieces of tortilla in batches until
nicely golden all over, removing and draining on paper towels as they are cooked.

2 Pour off all but a little oil from the pan and fry the onion in the remaining oil over
a low heat, stirring from time to time, until just beginning to color.

3 Add the meat and cook gently, stirring, until warmed through, 1 to 2 minutes.

4 Stir in the tortilla pieces and half the cheese, then sprinkle the top with the remaining cheese.
Cover the pan and place over a low heat for a few minutes until the cheese has melted. With the
tortillas, cooked meat, and cheese, you may not need any added seasoning.

*You can, of course, use ready-made tortilla chips for ease. Stirring in 2 or 3 beaten
eggs will turn it into something resembling a Spanish omelet type of tortilla.*

TRAIL DRIVE GRAVY

Makes about 2½ cups (600 ml)

3 tbsp. meat drippings or lard   18 fl. oz./2¼ cups (500 ml)
5 tbsp. flour   evaporated milk

1 In a heavy-duty pan, heat the drippings or lard over moderate heat, then stir in the flour and cook, stirring, for a few minutes until the flour is lightly browned.

2 Stir in the milk and about ½ cup (125 ml) water. Bring to a boil, stirring constantly, and simmer until the gravy is thick and smooth. Season to taste.

3 Serve with biscuits (page 24) or bread.

You can replace some or all of the evaporated milk with flat beer for a beer gravy. A wide range of flavorings can be added, such as chili, Tabasco sauce, fresh herbs, Worcestershire sauce, and more.

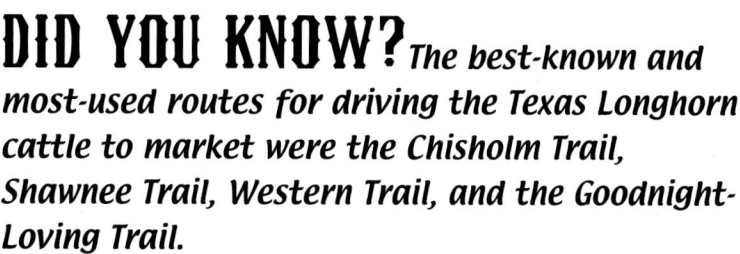

DID YOU KNOW? The best-known and most-used routes for driving the Texas Longhorn cattle to market were the Chisholm Trail, Shawnee Trail, Western Trail, and the Goodnight-Loving Trail.

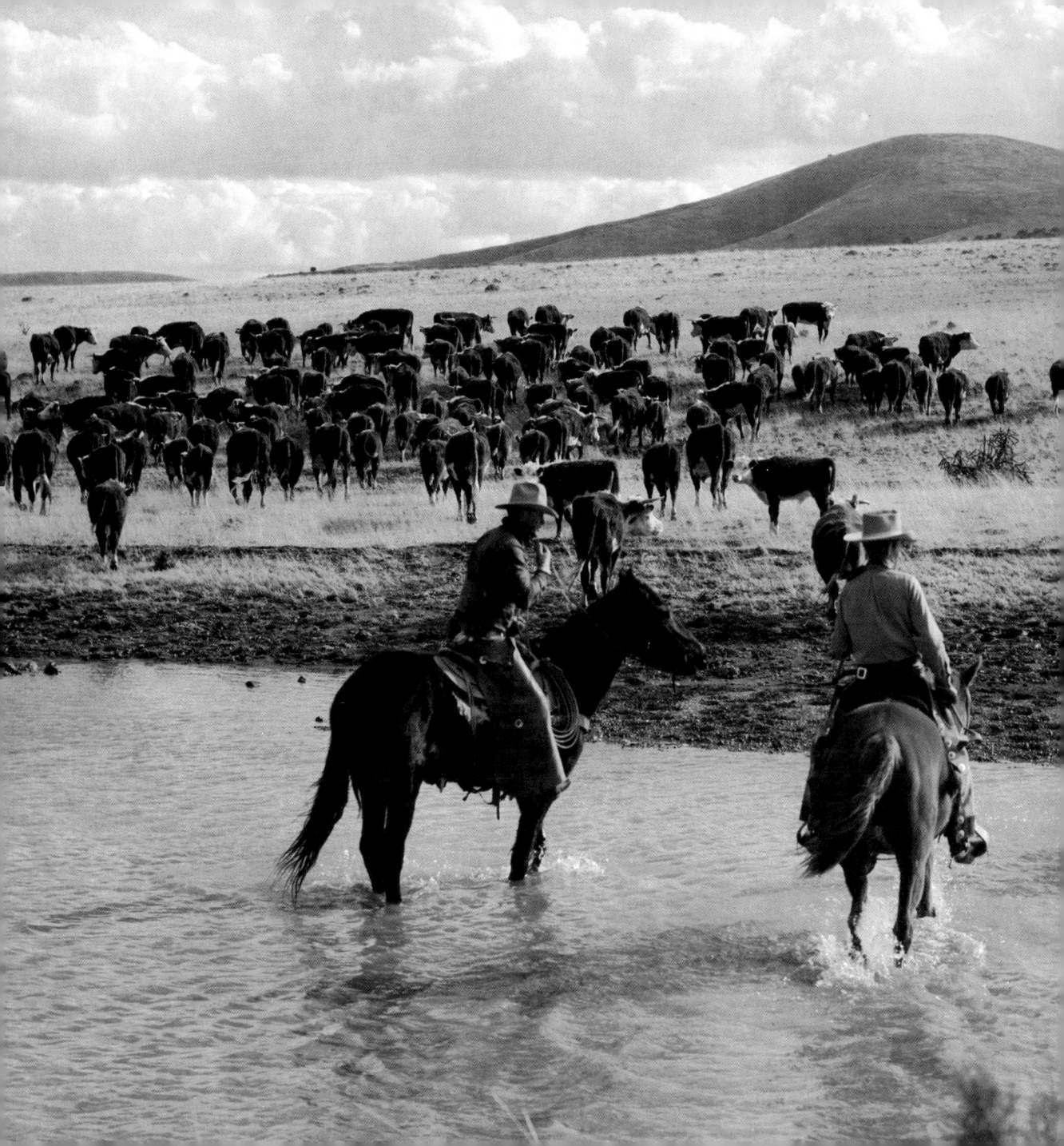

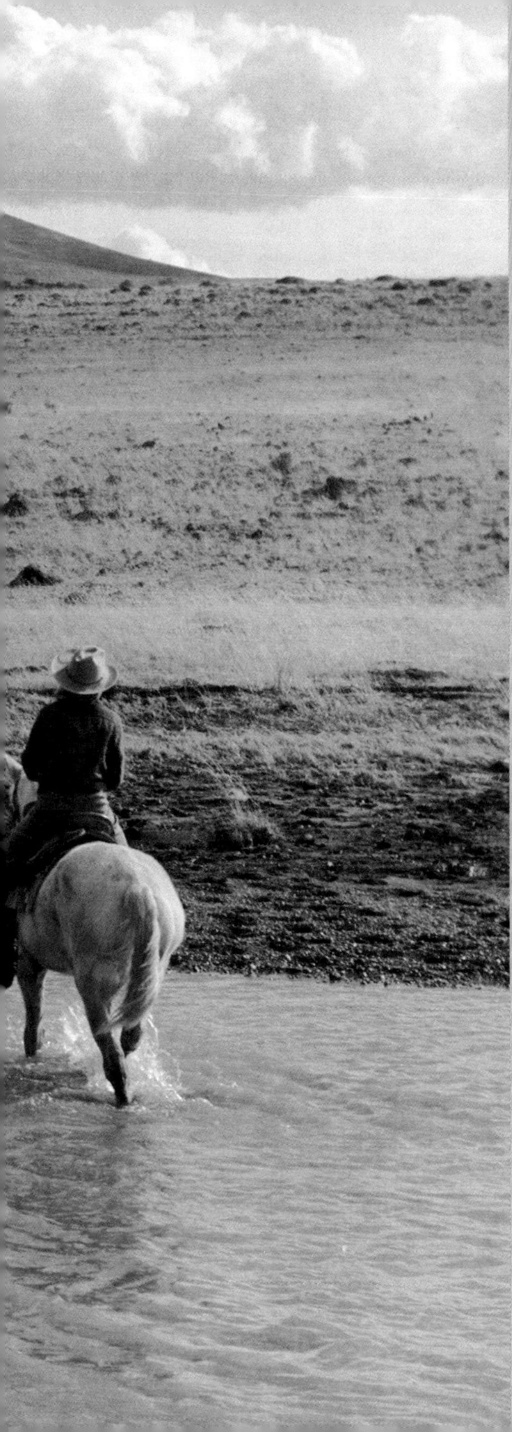

"*IT WAS A LAND OF VAST SILENT SPACES, OF LONELY RIVERS, AND OF PLAINS WHERE THE WILD GAME STARED AT THE PASSING HORSEMAN. IT WAS A LAND OF SCATTERED RANCHES, OF HERDS OF LONG-HORNED CATTLE, AND OF RECKLESS RIDERS...*"

Theodore Roosevelt
FROM AN AUTOBIOGRAPHY; "IV: IN COWBOY LAND"

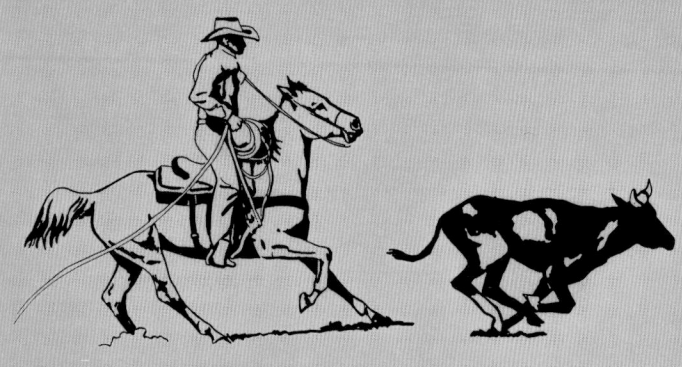

The Old Chisholm Trail

Well, come along boys and listen to my tale
I'll tell you of my troubles on the old Chisholm trail.

Chorus:
Come a ti yi yippy yippy yay, yippy yay
Come a ti yi yippy yippy yay

With a ten-dollar horse and a forty-dollar saddle,
I started in herdin' these Texas cattle **(Chorus)**

I'm up in the mornin' afore daylight
And afore I sleep the moon shines bright **(Chorus)**

Oh it's bacon and beans most every day
We'll soon be eating this prairie hay **(Chorus)**

With my seat in the saddle and my hand on the horn
I'm the best cowpuncher that ever was born **(Chorus)**

It's cloudy in the west, a-lookin' like rain
And my durned old slicker's in the wagon again **(Chorus)**

No chaps, no slicker, and it's pourin' down rain
I swear I'll never night-herd again **(Chorus)**

Feet in the stirrups and seat in the saddle,
I hung and rattled with them long-horn cattle **(Chorus)**

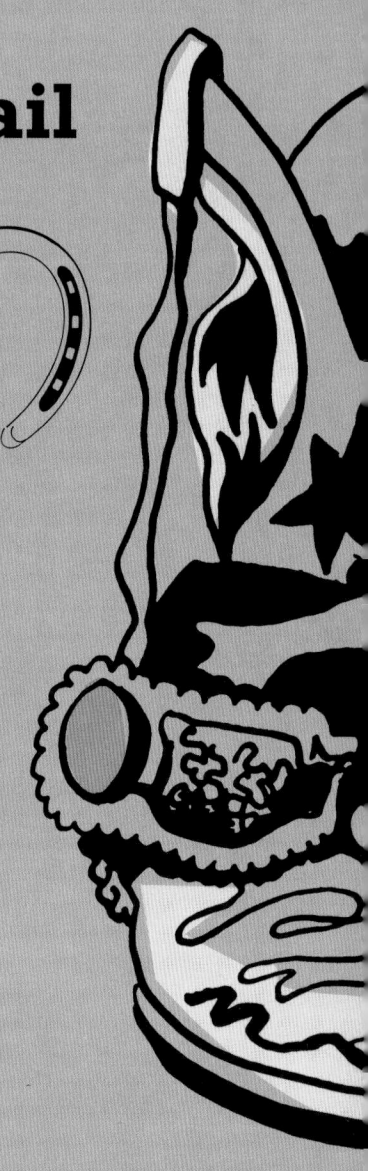

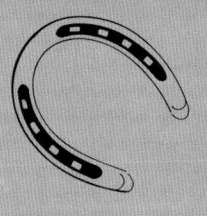

A stray in the herd and the boss said "Kill it!"
So I shot it in the rump with the handle of a skillet **(Chorus)**

I went to the boss to draw my roll,
And he had me figured out nine dollars in the hole **(Chorus)**

Me and my boss we had a little spat
So I hit him in the face with my ten gallon hat **(Chorus)**

I'm goin' to sell my horse, goin' to sell my saddle
'Cause I'm tired of punchin' these Longhorn cattle **(Chorus)**

Goin' back to town to draw my money,
Goin' back home to see my honey **(Chorus)**

With my knees in the saddle and my seat in the sky
I'll quit punchin' cows in the sweet by-and-by. **(Chorus)**

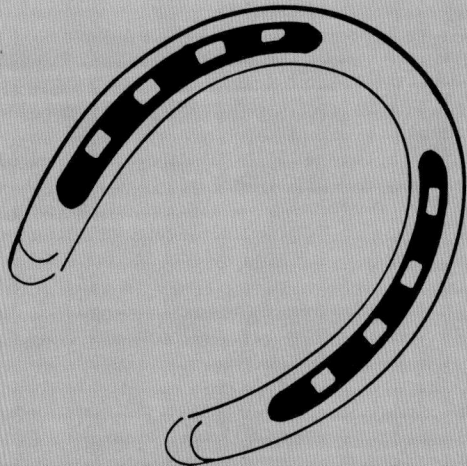

CORN CHOWDER

Serves 6–8

Cooking the corn first on a fire or barbecue, like Campfire Corn (page 55), will give the soup an extra full, delicious flavor. If no fresh milk is available, diluted evaporated milk can be used, or the potatoes mashed to give a creamy texture before adding the corn.

½ lb. (225 g) salt pork or thick-cut fatty bacon, finely diced
1 large onion, chopped
2–3 celery stalks, chopped (optional)
½ lb. (200 g) potatoes, diced
1 dried bay leaf

pinch of paprika (optional)
3 tbsp. flour
1½ cups (450 ml) milk
2 cups (450 g) (approx. 4 medium ears) freshly scraped corn or one 15-oz. can corn, drained.

1 In a large heavy pot, fry the pork or bacon until golden brown and the fat has run. Add the onion and celery and sauté until softened.

2 Add the potatoes with 2 cups of water, the bay leaf, paprika if using, and seasoning to taste. Bring to a boil, then lower the heat and simmer until the potatoes are soft, about 15 to 20 minutes.

3 Mix the flour with about one-quarter of the milk. Add to the pot and stir until well blended. Simmer for about 5 minutes. At the same time, heat the rest of the milk in a separate pan.

4 Add the hot milk and corn to the soup and warm through gently, but don't allow to boil. Adjust the seasoning and remove the bay leaf before serving.

You can give this a modern lift by adding some diced red pepper with the potatoes and a good handful of chopped coriander with the corn.

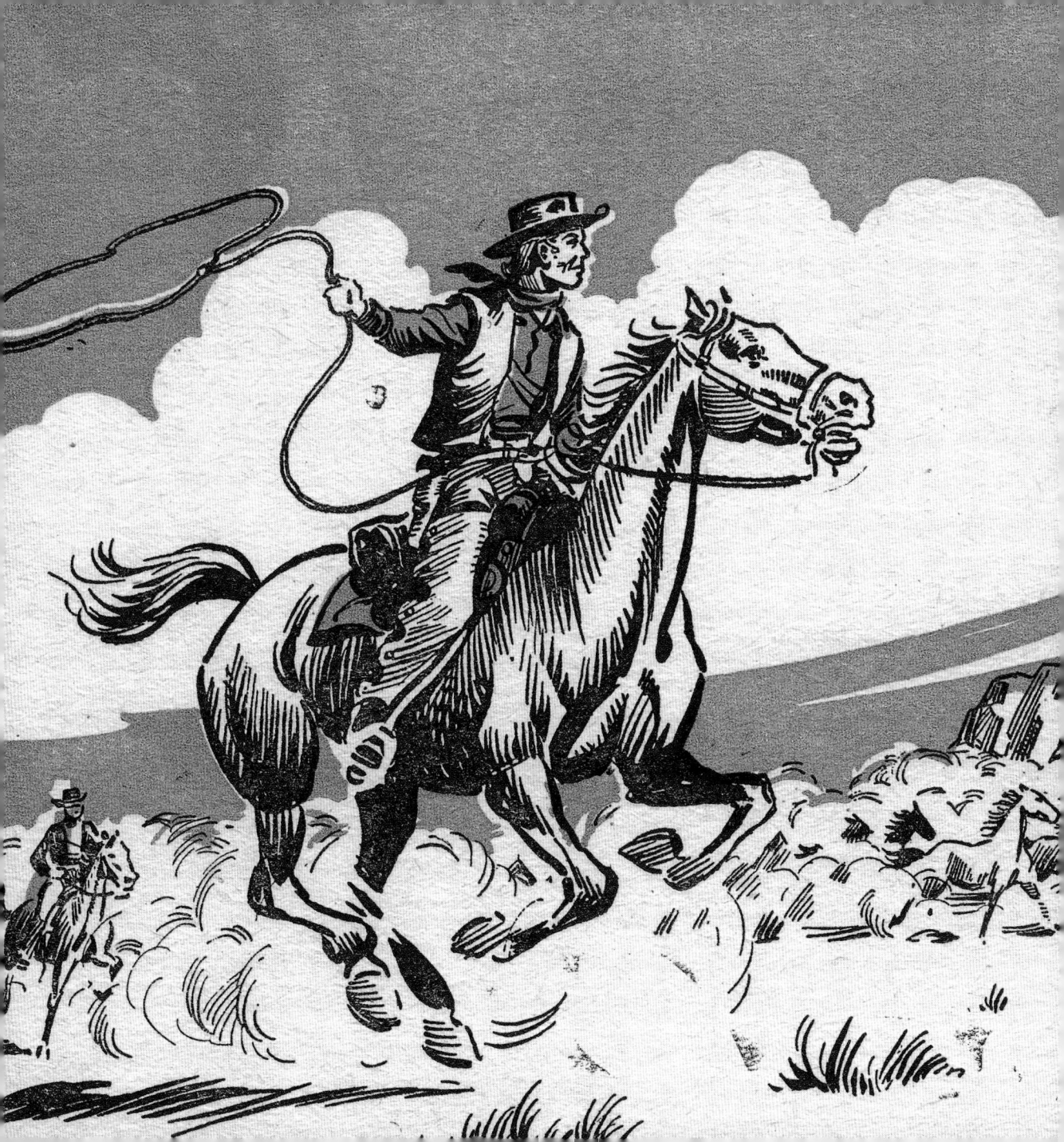

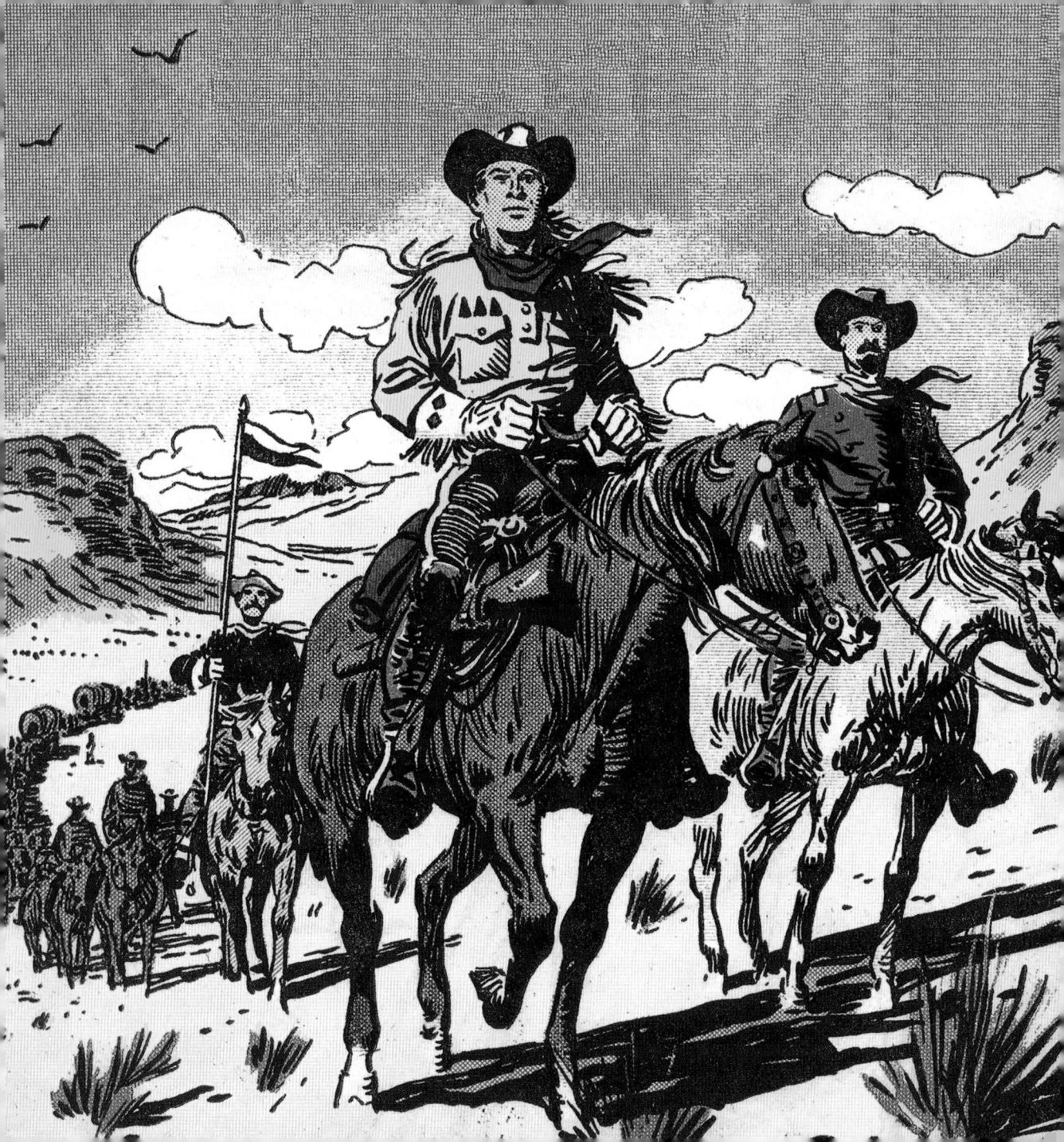

BEAN SOUP WITH DUMPLINGS

Serves 4

7 oz. (200 g) dried beans, soaked overnight (you can use navy, kidney, or black beans)
6 oz. (175 g) dried or salt pork or slab bacon, diced
½ bay leaf (optional)
1 tsp. sugar
1½ tbsp. oil

1½ tbsp. flour

For the dumplings:
1 egg
3 oz./⅓ cup (85g) flour
large pinch of salt
4–5 tbsp. water

1 Drain the soaked beans and place in a large pan with fresh cold water to cover generously. Add the pork or bacon, bay leaf if using, and the sugar, and bring to a boil, then reduce the heat and simmer gently for about 2 hours.

2 Heat the oil in a frying pan over a low heat and stir in the flour. Keep stirring until it starts to turn brown and smell nutty (this will take up to 30 minutes)—do not let the flour burn. Add a little bean liquid to thin, stirring well. Pour into the pot of beans and mix well. Let this simmer.

3 Make the dumplings: Beat the egg in a bowl and stir in the other ingredients. Beat until batter is stiff.

4 Bring the bean soup to a boil (you may have to add some more water to get a good soup consistency), lower the heat, and drop in large spoonfuls of the batter. Cook gently for about 15 minutes. Adjust the seasoning before serving.

You can, if you like, flavor the dumplings with grated nutmeg, finely chopped fresh herbs if you have them, grated onion, or shredded cheese.

TRAIL SOUP

Serves 6

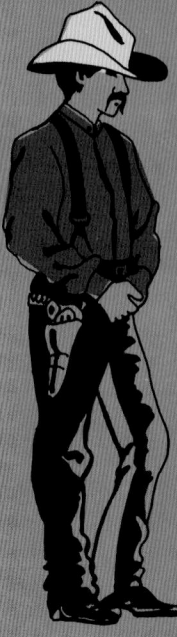

10 oz. (300 g) dried beans, ideally
a mix of equal parts navy, pinto,
anasazi or canellini, black
beans, and red kidney beans
2 tbsp. oil
1 large onion, chopped
2 celery stalks, chopped

2 large carrots, chopped
2 garlic cloves, chopped
1 bay leaf
3½ pints/7 cups (1½ liters) beef,
chicken, or vegetable stock
or water

1 Soak the beans in water overnight.

2 Heat the oil in a large pot and sauté the onion, celery, carrots, and garlic until soft. Add the drained beans, bay leaves, and stock or water. Bring to a boil, lower the heat, and simmer for 2 to 3 hours, or until all the beans are tender.

3 Season to taste and serve.

"All in all, my years on the trail were the happiest I ever lived. There were many hardships and dangers, of course, that called on all a man had of endurance and bravery; but when all went well there was no other life so pleasant. Most of the time we were solitary adventurers in a great land as fresh and new as a spring morning, and we were free and full of the zest of darers."

Charles Goodnight, Texas rancher, quoted by Geoffrey C. Ward in
THE WEST, AN ILLUSTRATED HISTORY.

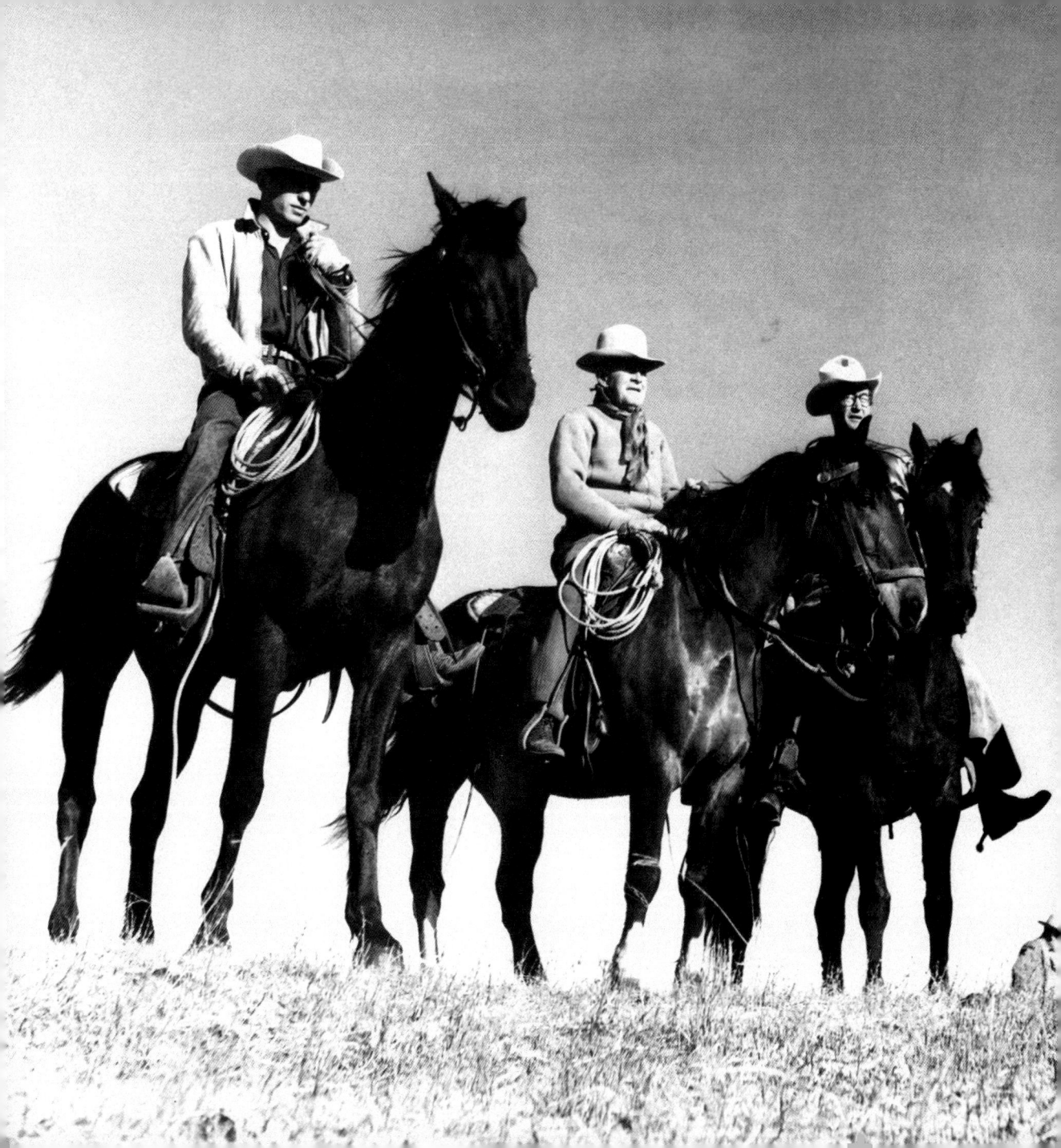

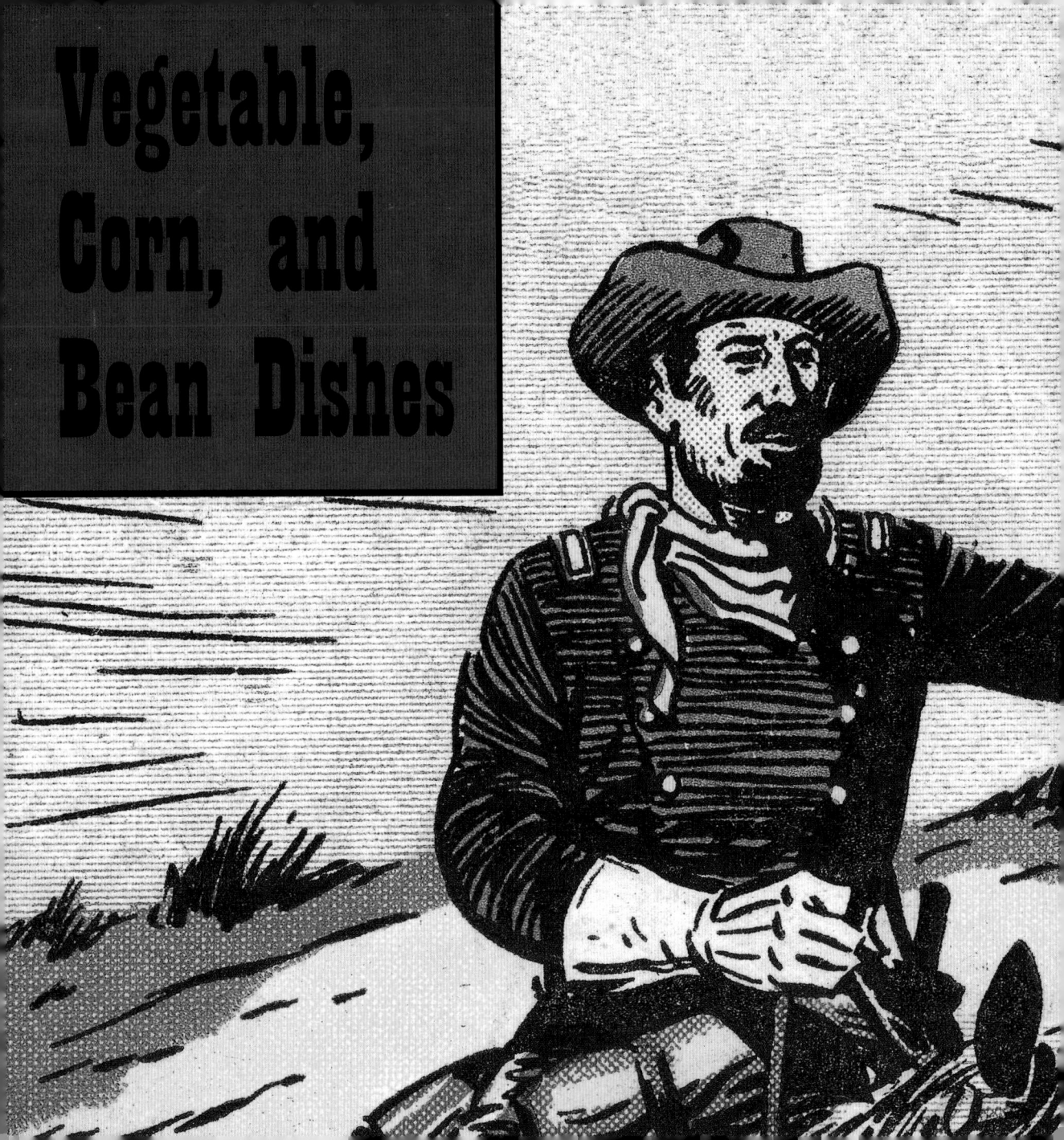

Vegetable,
Corn, and
Bean Dishes

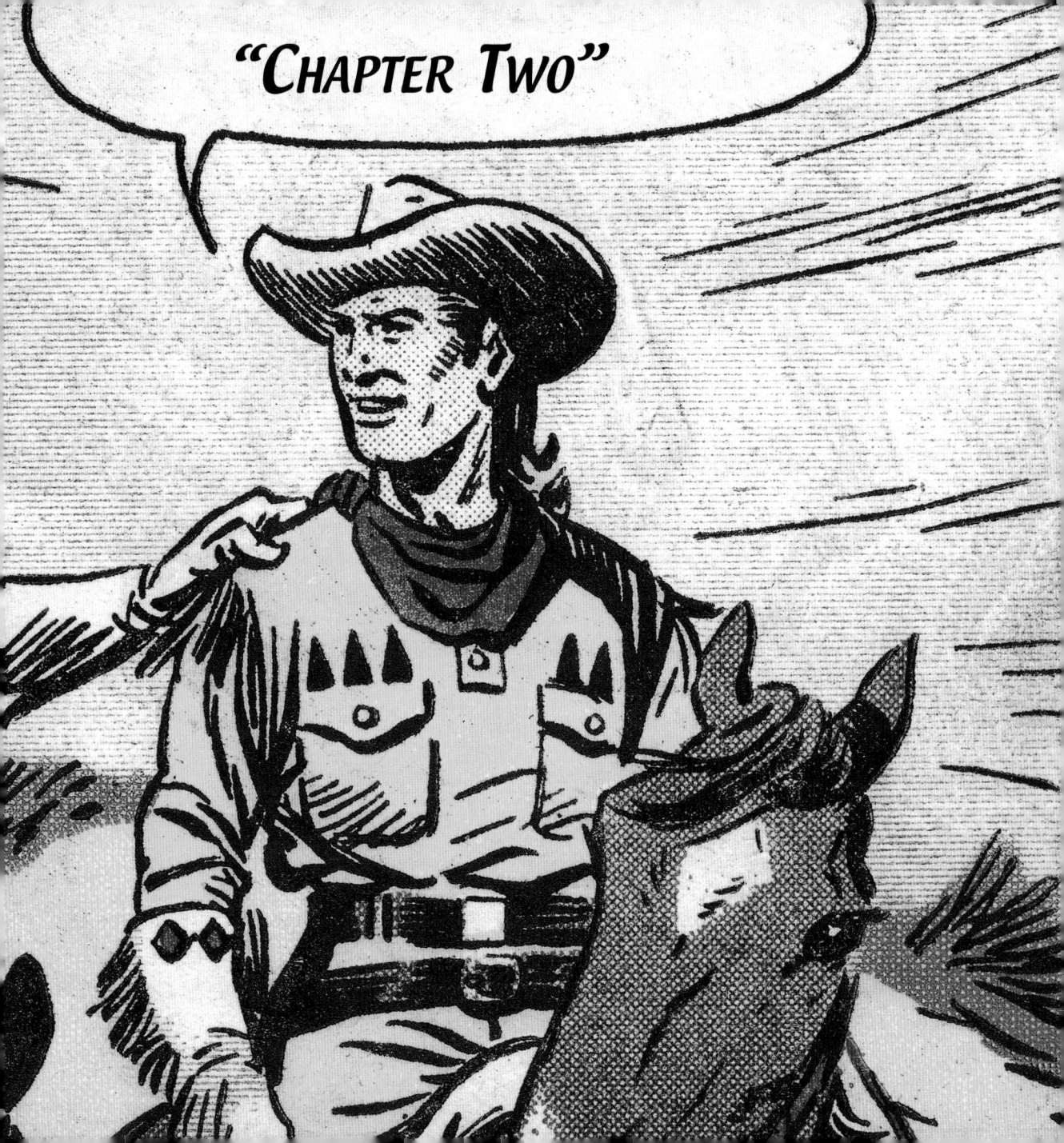

*O*ther than potatoes and onions, vegetables were a scarce commodity on the trail and were among the foods the cowboys would descend upon hungrily whenever they hit town and could choose what they ate.

There were, of course, some wild vegetables like prairie peas and wild greens to be found, but they took a deal of foraging, so greens generally remained a considerable luxury. Dried sliced vegetables were often among the supplies carried in the chuck wagon but, by all accounts, these were often in such poor condition they were regarded with considerable disdain and reserved for the stewpot.

In place of greens, there was always corn in many guises, together with a wide variety of beans. Both corn and beans were invaluable on the trail as they could be preserved in ways that not only kept them in a fairly good condition for eating but also retained a considerable amount of their nutrients. Together, they supplied complete protein.

The cook could also pick up more of both of these essential supplies on the trail, and could even learn new ways of preparing them from the native Americans and the "vaqueros," the Mexican herdsmen who were the cowboys' predecessors.

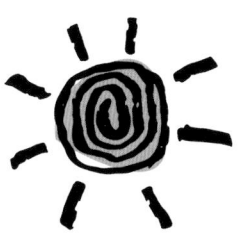

SUCCOTASH

Serves 4

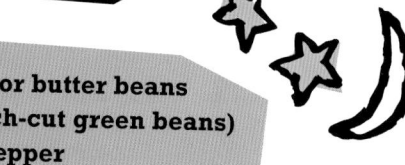

1 oz./2 tbsp. (25 g) butter
14 oz./1¾ cups (400 g) cooked or
canned corn kernels, drained
14 oz./1¾ cup (400 g) cooked or
canned lima beans, drained

(or fava or butter beans
or French-cut green beans)
salt and pepper
½ tsp. paprika

1 Melt the butter in a heavy-duty pan and add the corn and beans with salt and pepper to taste and the paprika. Mix gently over a very low heat until everything is warmed through.

If you have it, some chopped parsley added just before serving really sets this off, and a few spoonfuls of sour cream gives it a luxurious feeling.

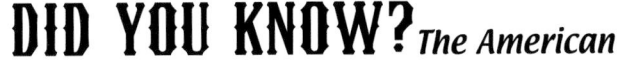

DID YOU KNOW? *The American Indians introduced the colonists and cowboys to this bean and corn dish. Its name comes from the Narragansett word "msickquatash" meaning "boiled whole kernels of corn."*

Chuckwagon Etiquette

These unwritten rules were strictly followed by the trail crew:

1. No one eats until Cookie calls.
2. When Cookie calls, everyone comes a runnin'.
3. Hungry cowboys wait for no man. They fill their plates, fill their bellies, then move on so stragglers can fill their plates.
4. Cowboys eat first, talk later.
5. It's okay to eat with your fingers. The food is clean.
6. Eat with your hat on.
7. Don't take the last serving unless you're sure you're the last man.
8. Food left on the plate is an insult to the cook.
9. Don't even think of going back to work without putting your dishes in the wreck pan.
10. No running or saddling a horse near the wagon. And when you ride off, always ride down wind from the wagon.
11. If you enjoy the water bucket, refill it—pronto.
12. If you're refilling the coffee cup and someone yells "Man at the pot," you're obliged to serve refills.
13. If you come across any decent firewood, bring it back to the wagon.
14. If you ride by the campfire and Cookie's nowhere in sight, stop and stir the beans.
15. Strangers are always welcome at the wagon.

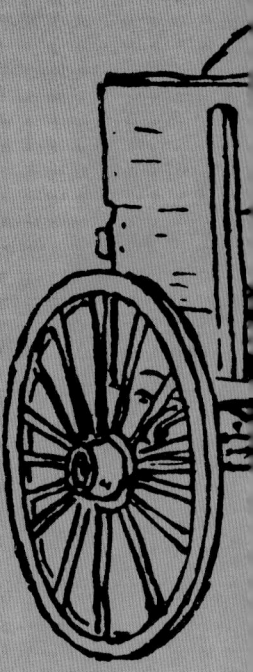

FROM THE COWBOY LIFE; A SADDLEBAG GUIDE FOR DUDES, TENDERFEET, AND COW PUNCHERS EVERYWHERE by Michelle Morris

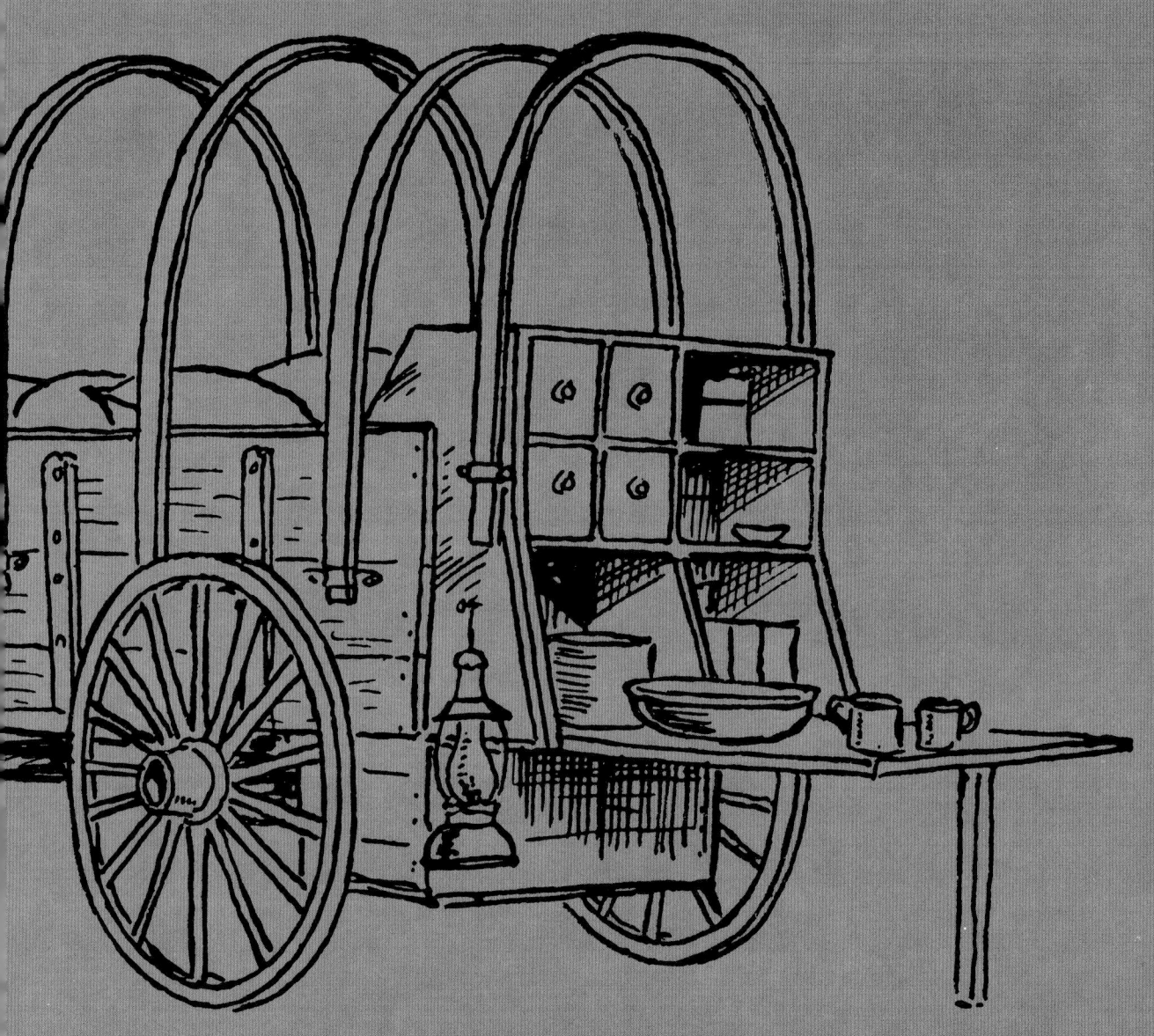

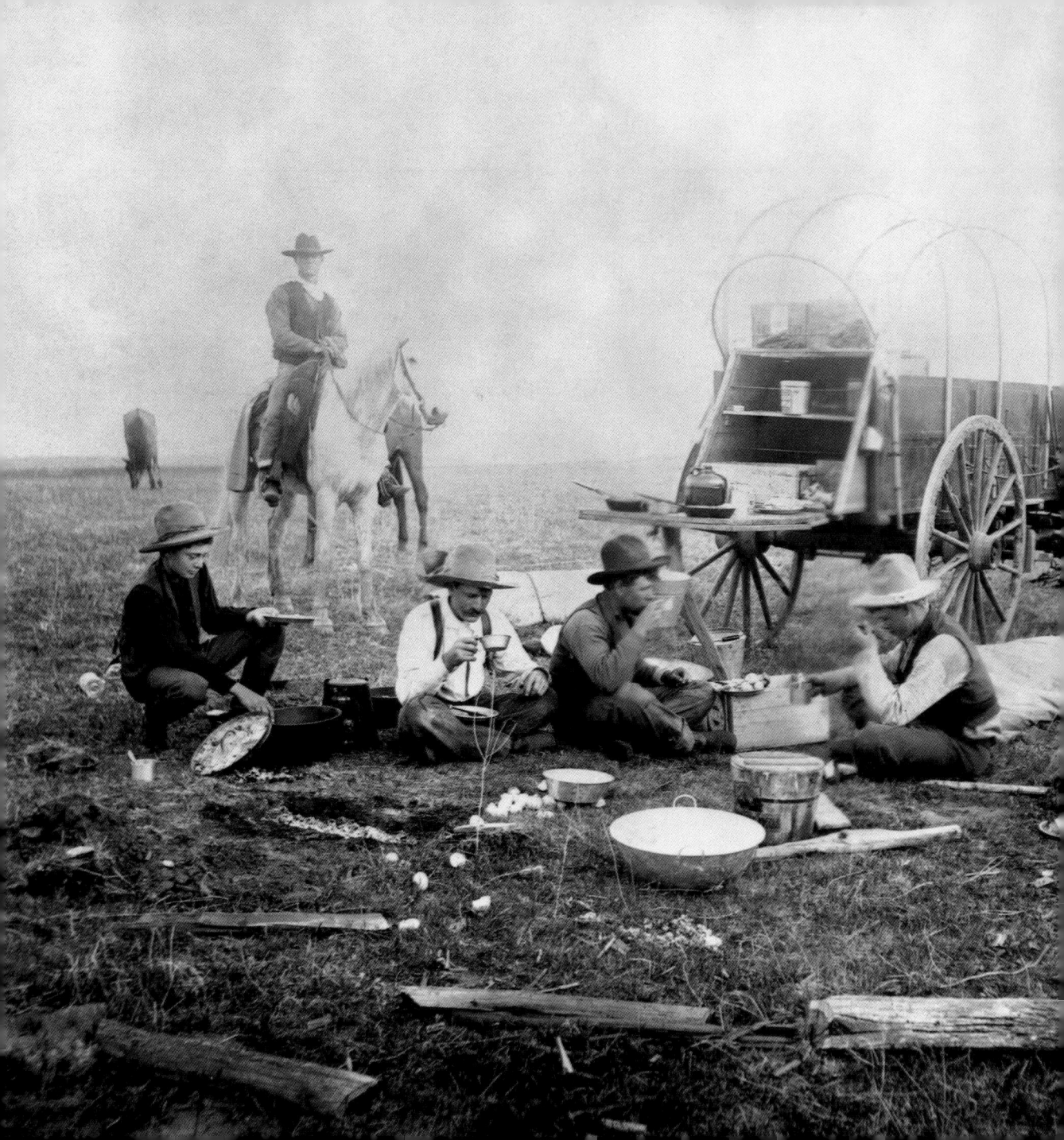

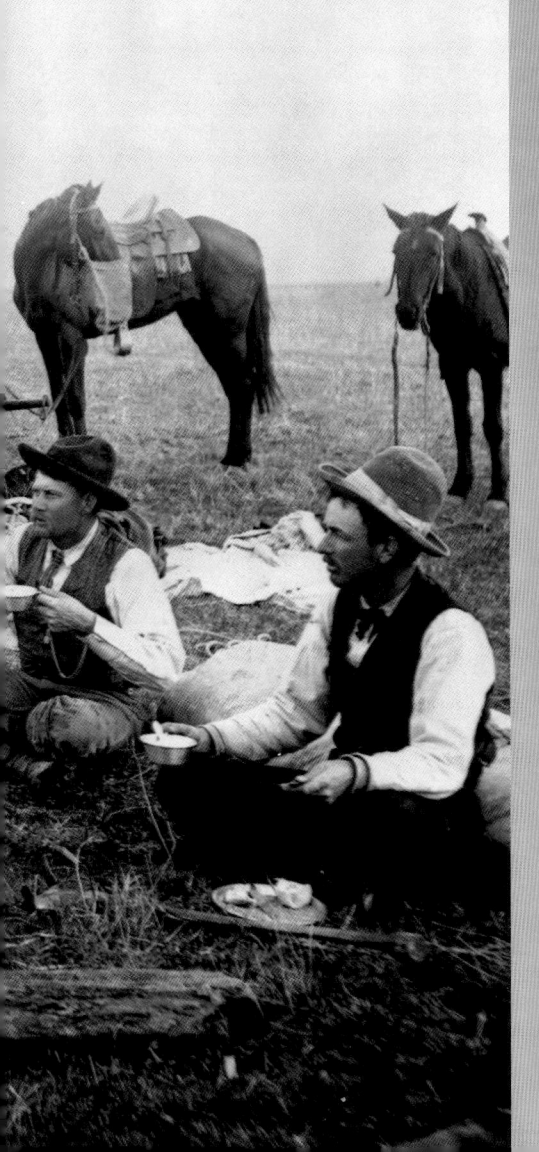

"*THE SUPPER WAS A SUCCESS, NOT ON ACCOUNT OF THE SPREAD OR OUR SUPERIOR TABLE MANNERS, BUT WE GRACED THE OCCASION WITH APPETITES WHICH REQUIRED THE STAPLES OF LIFE TO SATISFY.*"

Andy Adams, cowboy, 1905
FROM THE OUTLET

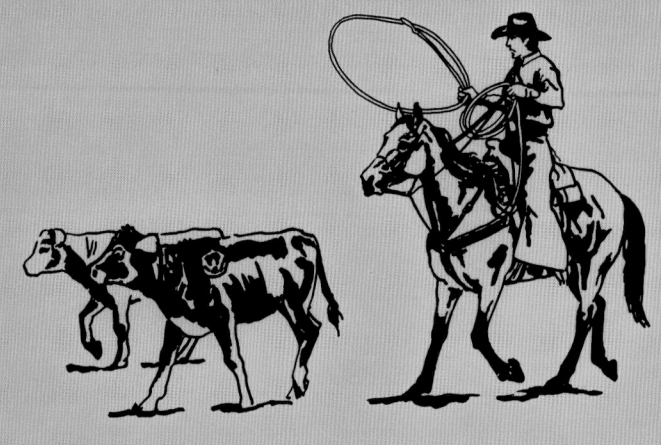

CORN OYSTERS

Makes about 16

10 oz. (275 g) freshly scraped, defrosted frozen, or canned corn kernels, drained
2 eggs, separated
3 oz. (85 g) flour
½ tsp. baking powder

large pinch of salt
freshly grated nutmeg to taste (optional)
oil, for frying
maple syrup, to serve (optional)

1 In a large bowl, mix all the ingredients except the egg whites, oil, and maple syrup.

2 Beat the eggs whites to soft peaks and then fold into the corn mixture.

3 Heat the oil and drop tablespoonfuls of batter into the oil a few at a time, turning them once, until golden on both sides.

4 Remove "oysters," drain on crumpled paper towels, and cover with aluminum foil to keep hot while the rest are being cooked. Serve as soon as they are all ready, with maple syrup if you like.

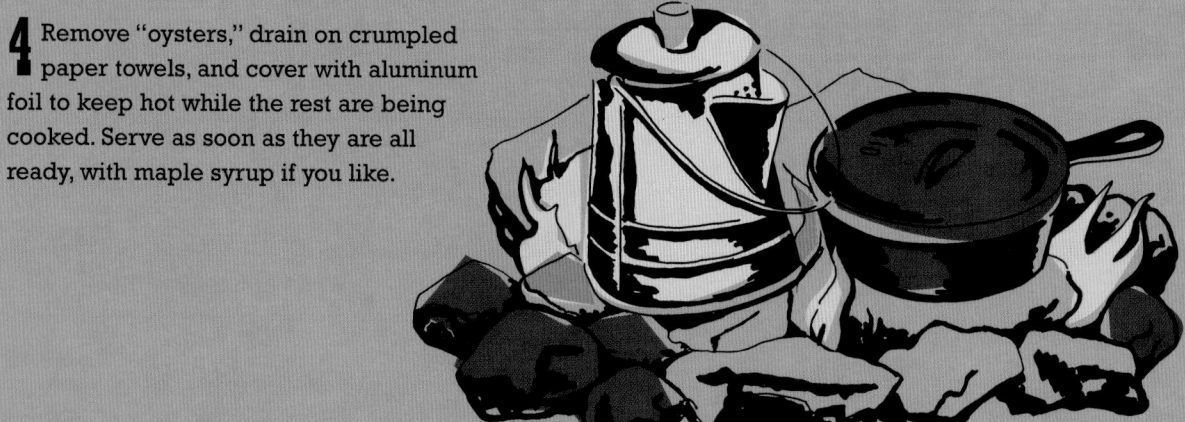

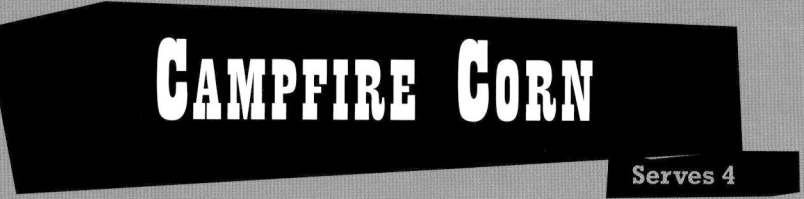

CAMPFIRE CORN

Serves 4

4 fresh ears of corn **about 2 oz./4 tbsp. (50g) butter**
2 lemons **salt and pepper**

1 Well ahead, pull out as much of the silk at the end of each cob as you can, but leave the corn in the husks. Soak the corn in cold water for at least an hour.

2 Drain the corn well and cook on the barbecue, turning from time to time, for about 30 minutes.

3 Remove the husks and serve with lemon halves for squeezing, some butter, and seasoning.

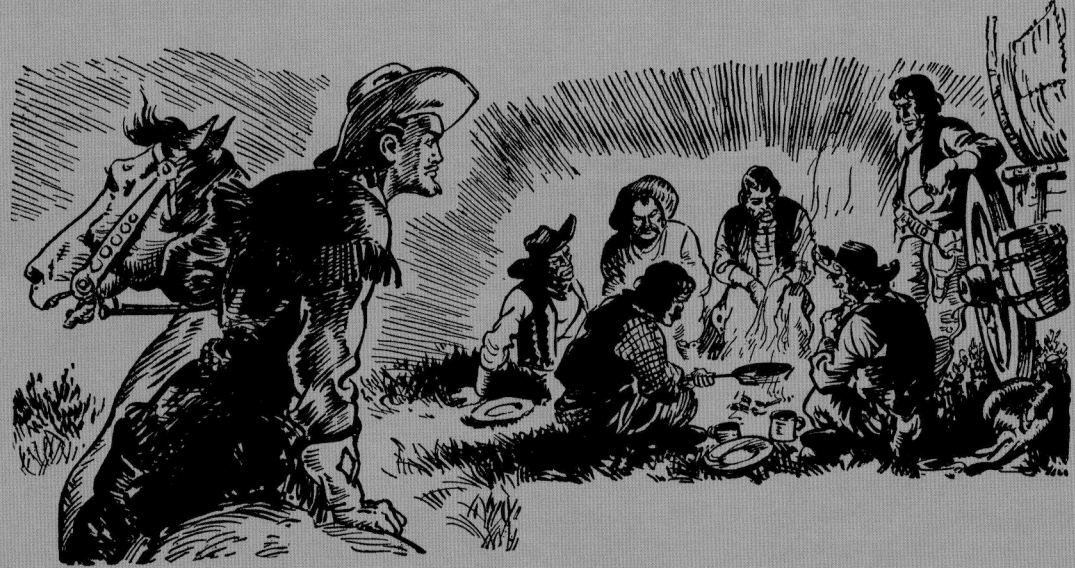

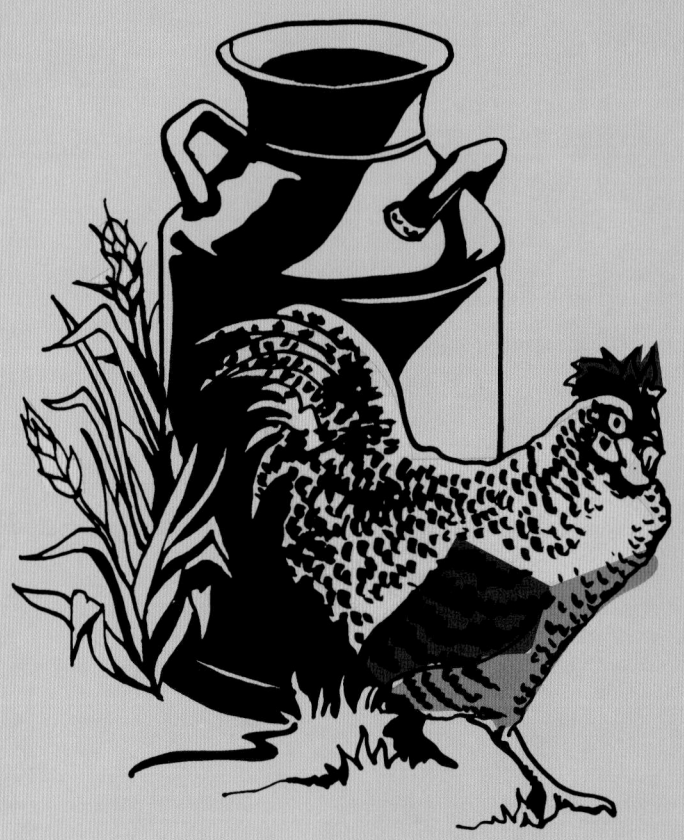

"Take the ears of Indian corn when in the Milk, and boil them almost enough to eat, then shell it, and spread it in a Cloth very thin, and dry it in the Sun till it shrinks to half its Bigness, and becomes very hard, then put it any dry Cask, and it will keep the Year round. When you use it, you must put it in a Pot, and let it warm moderately over a Fire for three to four Hours, but which Means it swells considerably, then boil it till you find 'tis fit to eat."

Benjamin Franklin's recipe for drying corn FROM BENJAMIN FRANKLIN BOOK OF RECIPES by Hilaire Dubourcq

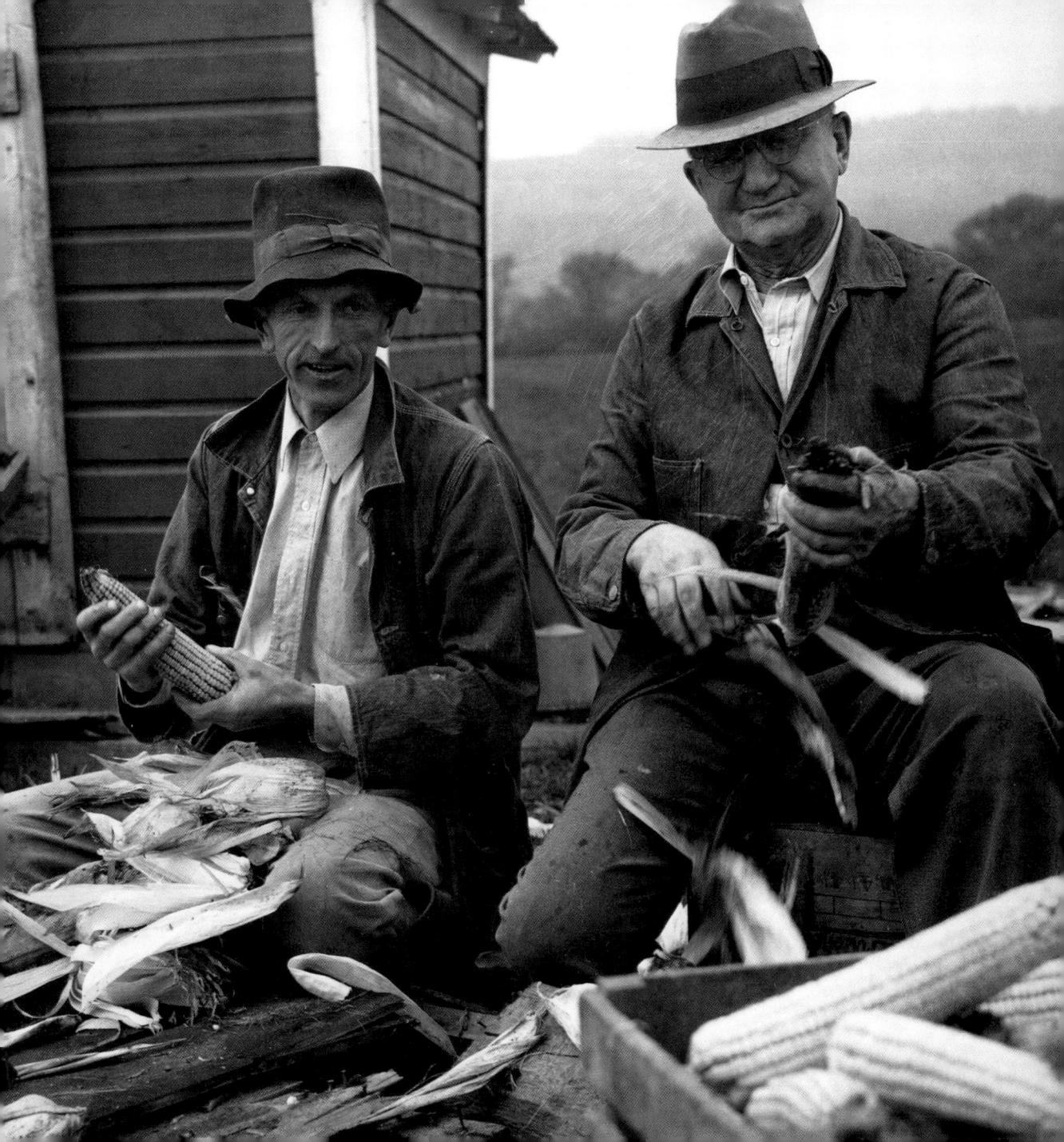

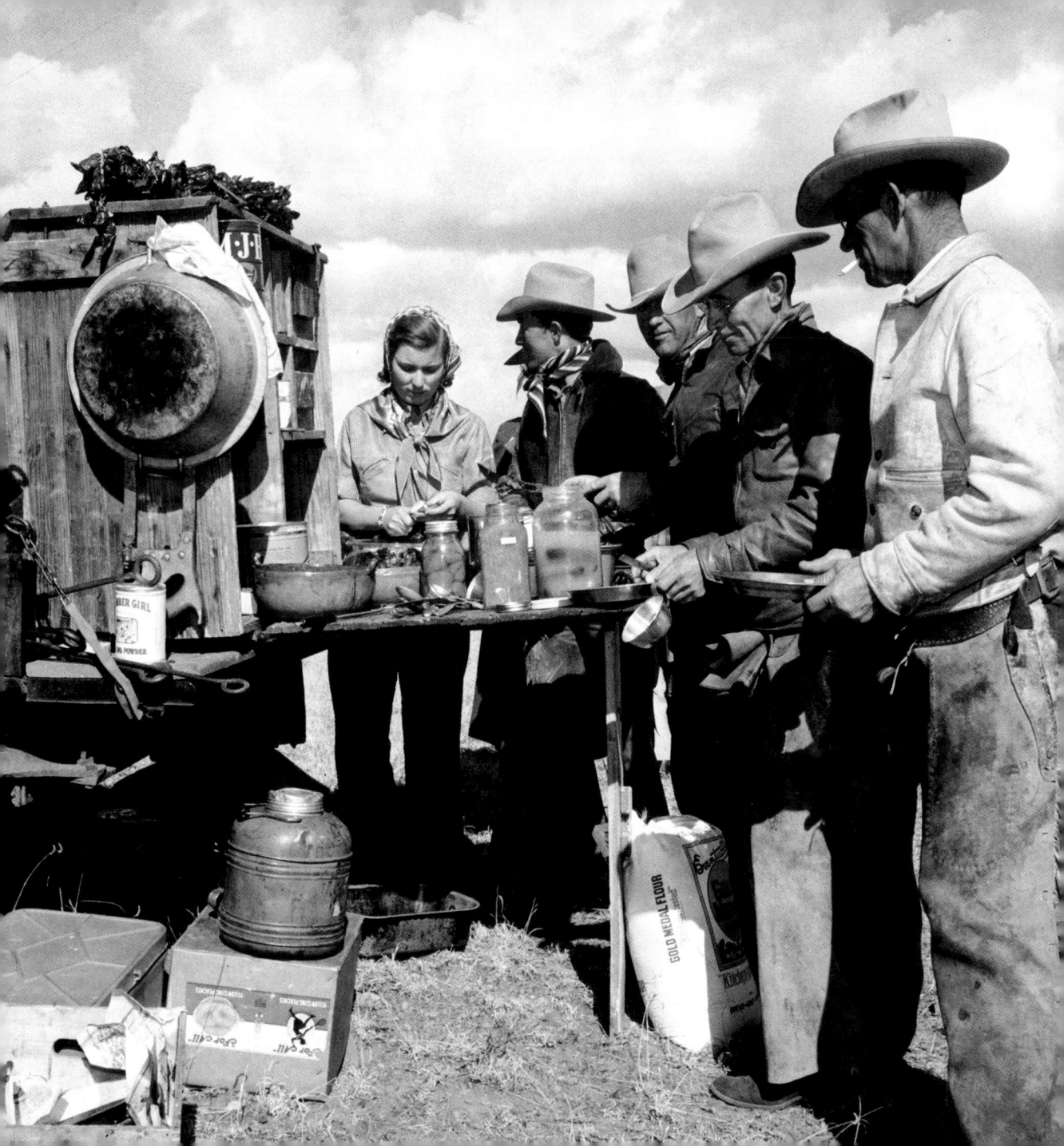

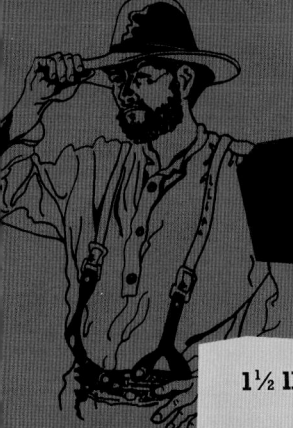

Pork 'n' Beans

Serves 6–8

1½ lb. (675 g) cooked beans, such as navy or kidney beans, or two 14-oz. (400-g) cans of beans, drained and rinsed
8 oz. (225 g) salt pork or fatty bacon, diced
1 onion, chopped
2 garlic cloves, finely chopped
4–6 tbsp. tomato ketchup
salt and pepper
4 oz. (125 g) cheddar cheese, grated (optional)

1 Fry the pork or bacon, stirring regularly, until the fat runs. Add the onion and garlic, and sauté until the onion is translucent. Remove the pan contents, leaving as much of the fat as possible

2 Add the beans to the pan and lightly mash them with a fork as you mix them with the hot fat.

3 Add the bacon and onion mixture back to the pan and mix with the beans, ketchup, and salt and pepper to taste. Add a little water if the mixture isn't creamy enough.

4 Cover, set over a very gentle heat, and cook until a crust forms on the bottom of the pan, about 1 hour.

5 Sprinkle with the cheese to serve (optional).

You can also add chopped chilies, chili flakes, or pepper sauce to taste.

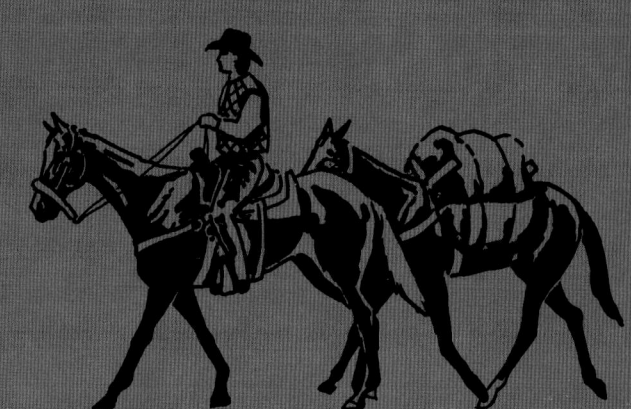

BBQ BEANS

Serves 6–8

4 oz. (115 g) salt pork or fatty bacon, diced
1½ lb. (675 g) cooked beans, such as navy and kidney beans, or two 14-oz. (400-g) cans of beans, drained and rinsed
1 onion, finely chopped
6–8 tbsp. tomato ketchup
1–2 tbsp. mustard
1 tbsp. Worcestershire sauce
1 tbsp. vinegar (cider, sherry, or white wine)
½ cup (150 ml) water
2–3 tbsp. dark brown sugar or molasses
3 garlic cloves, crushed

1 Fry the pork or bacon until browned and just crisp.

2 In a heavy-duty pot, mix the bacon and its fat with all the other ingredients, cover tightly, and place over a gentle heat for at least 2 hours, stirring once or twice and adding a little more water if it seems too dry.

Alcohol was usually forbidden on the trail, but you could try replacing the water with beer for a great modern alternative.

"They had a very little grub and they usually run out of that and lived on straight beef; they had only three or four horses to the man, mostly with sore backs; ... they had no tents, no tarps, and damn few slickers. They never kicked, because those boys was raised under just the same conditions as there was on the trail— corn meal and bacon for grub, dirt floors in the houses, and no luxuries."

Teddy Blue Abbott, cowboy, 1879, FROM WE POINTED THEM NORTH: RECOLLECTIONS OF A COWPUNCHER.

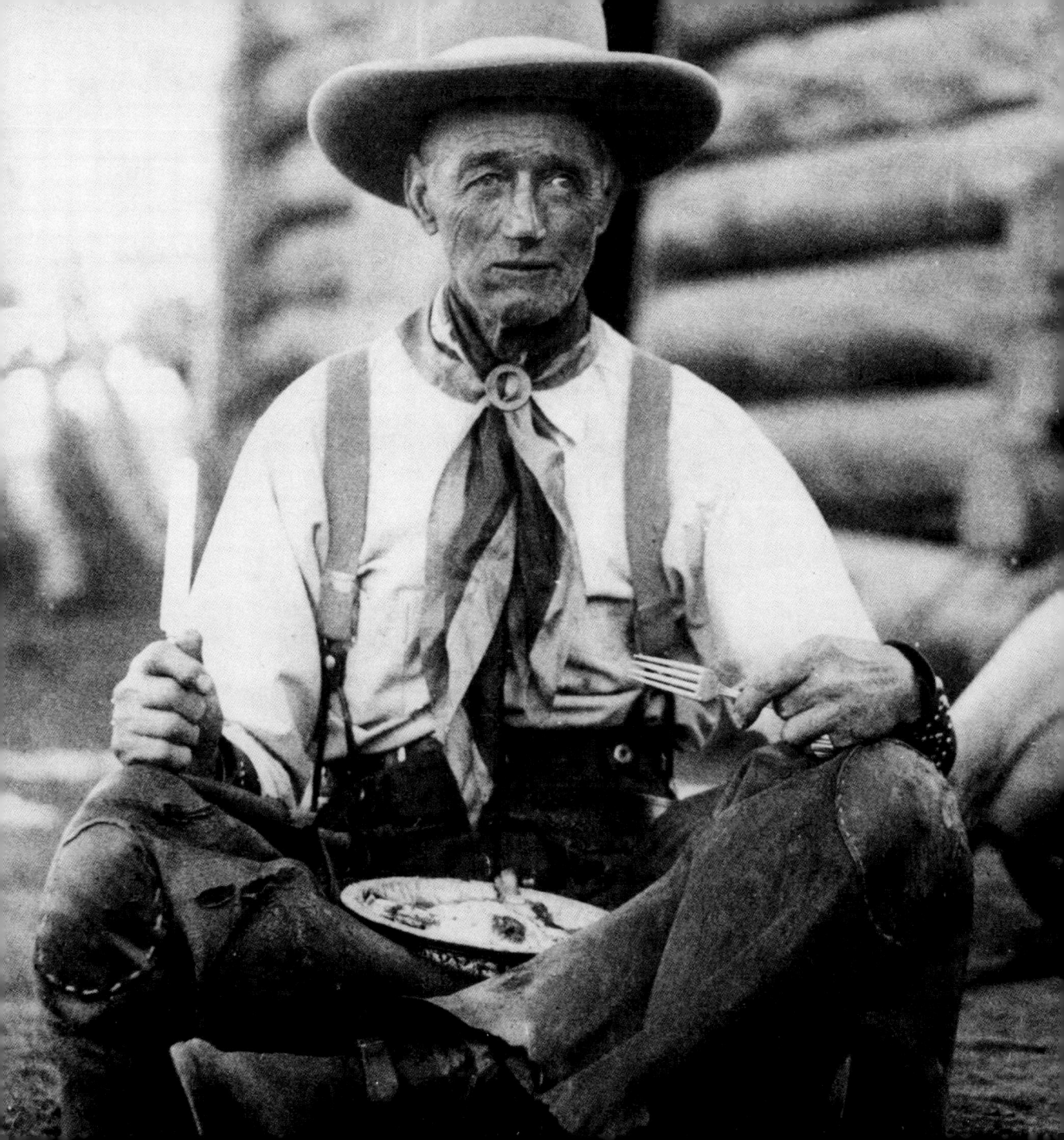

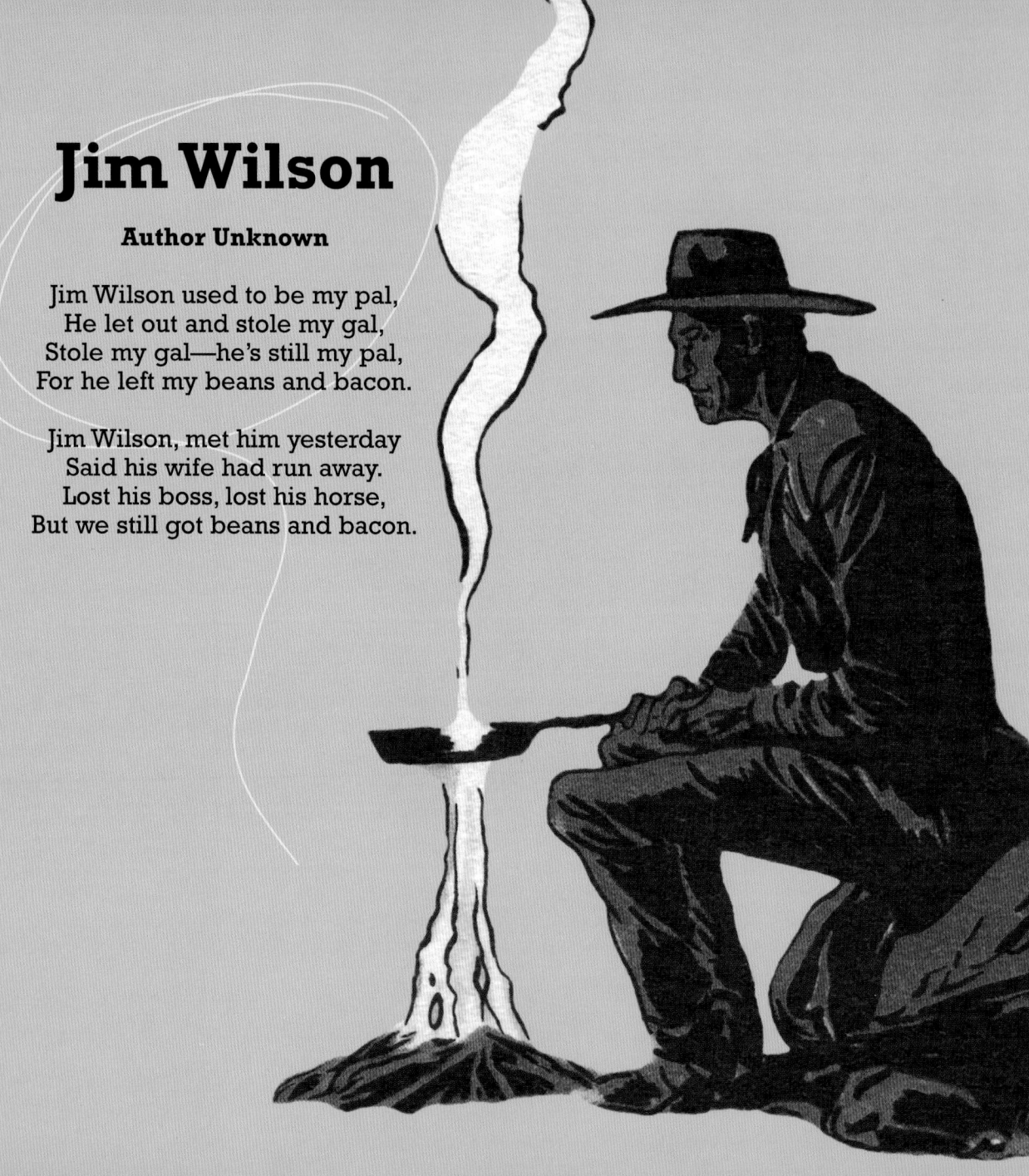

Jim Wilson

Author Unknown

Jim Wilson used to be my pal,
He let out and stole my gal,
Stole my gal—he's still my pal,
For he left my beans and bacon.

Jim Wilson, met him yesterday
Said his wife had run away.
Lost his boss, lost his horse,
But we still got beans and bacon.

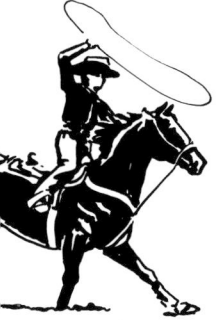

TEXAS CAVIAR

Serves 6–8

4 tbsp. olive oil
1 tbsp. vinegar (cider, sherry, or white wine)
several good splashes of Tabasco sauce
salt and pepper
1½ lb. (675 g) cooked black-eyed peas, or two 14-oz. (400-g) cans of black-eyed peas, drained and rinsed
4–5 scallions, chopped
3 large tomatoes, finely chopped
2 tbsp. chopped coriander leaves (optional)

1 First make the dressing by mixing the oil, vinegar, and Tabasco (more or less, depending on how hot you like your food). Season to taste with salt and pepper.

2 Mix the remaining ingredients in a salad bowl and toss with the dressing.

DID YOU KNOW? *Cowboy slang terms for beans include Pecos strawberries, Texas strawberries, whistle berries, prairie whistlers, and frijoles (pronounced "free-holy").*

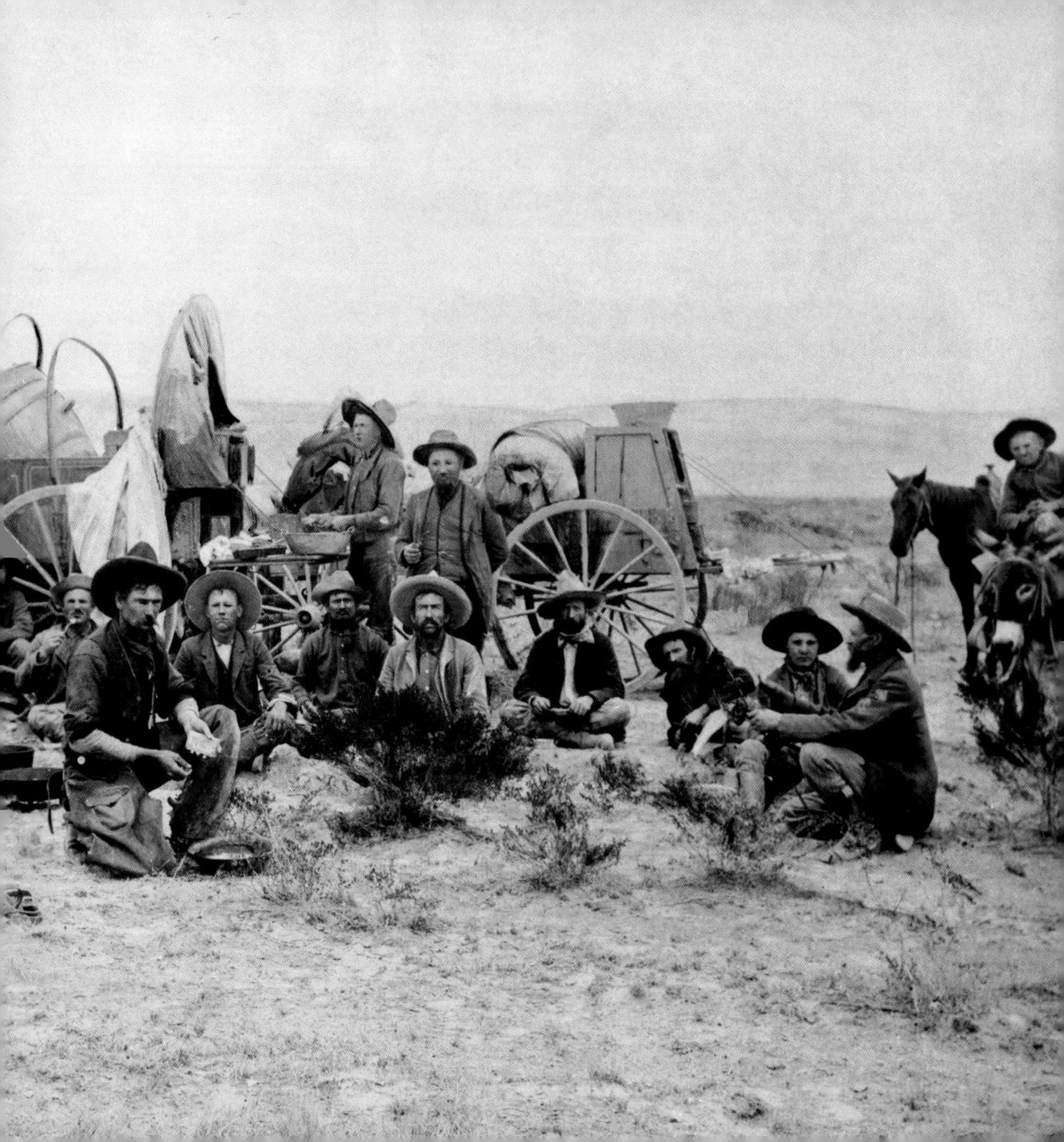

The Old Dutch Oven

by Arthur Chapman

Some sigh for cooks of boyhood days, but none of them for me;
One roundup cook was best of all—'t was with the X-Bart-T.
And when we heard the grub-pile call at morning, noon, and night,
The old Dutch oven never failed to cook the things just right.

'T was covered o'er with red-hot coals, and when we fetched her out,
The biscuits there were of the sort no epicure would flout.
I ain't so strong for boyhood grub, 'cause, summer, spring, or fall,
The old Dutch oven backed the stuff that tasted best of all.

Perhaps 't was 'cause our appetites were always mighty sharp—
The men who ride the cattle range ain't apt to kick or carp:
But, anyway, I find myself a-dreaming of that bread
The old Dutch oven backed for us beneath those coals so red.

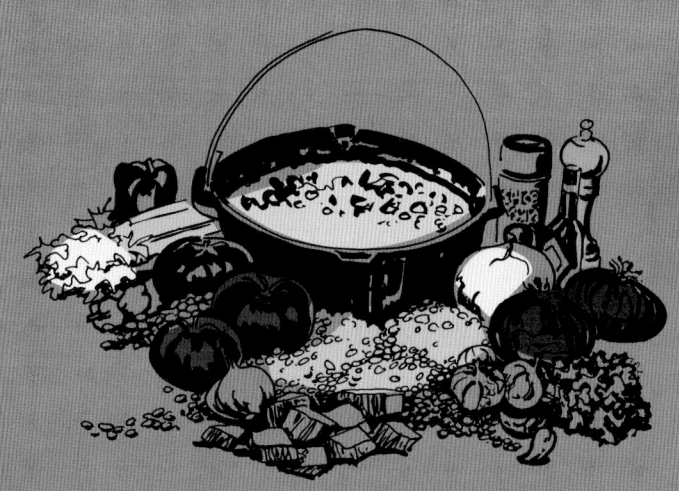

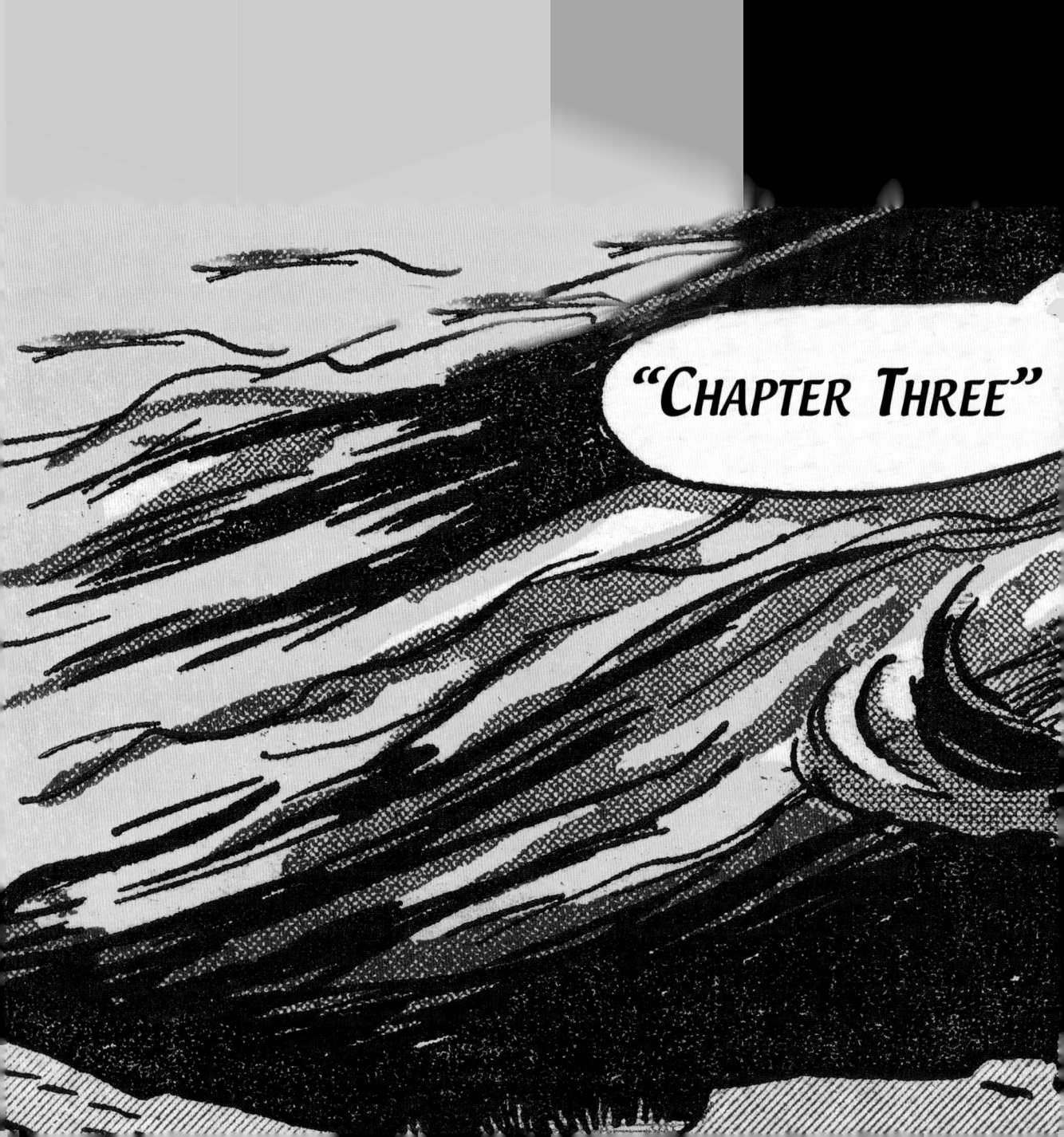

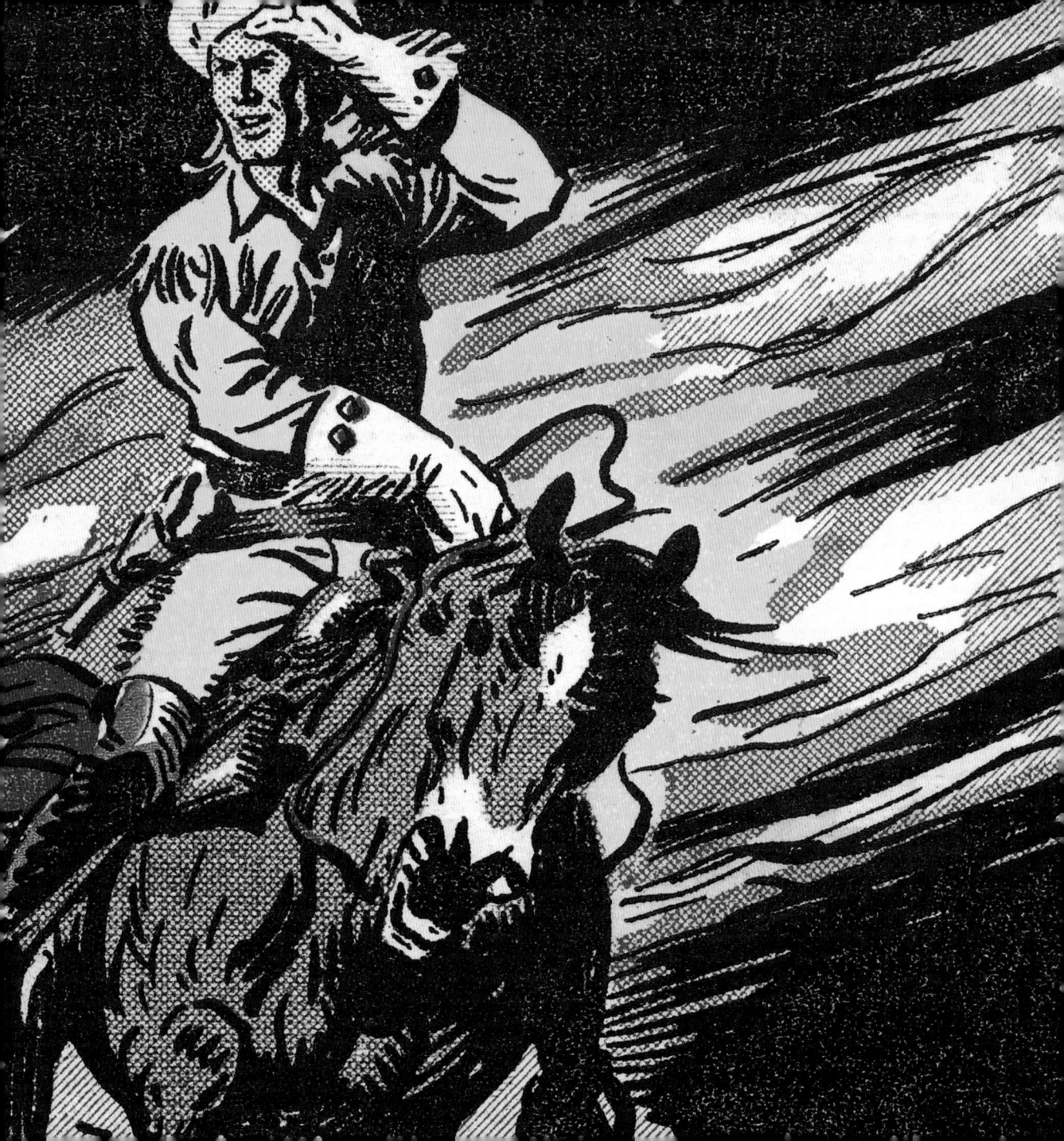

*A*part from dried meats, like jerky, meat for the cowboys tended to be beef from weaker cattle that were obviously not going to survive the journey, or from strays left behind by other trail herds. Other meats came from wild creatures like antelope, deer, rabbits, and game birds such as pheasant that they happened across along the way. Hunting was the only way many cowboys could survive the off-seasons, when they were on the ranch, rather than on the trail.

The cook was usually quite a skilled butcher and could differentiate which cuts were naturally tender and suited rapid cooking directly over the fire and which needed long slow stewing or braising in a pot or Dutch oven to get them tender.

Meat was normally stewed with the few vegetables they had on hand, or dried vegetable cake, and often only salt and pepper as seasoning. However, some cooks did have knowledge of the wild herbs that grew on the plains and used them to enhance the flavor of their meat dishes—sometimes even coffee was used for added taste. Meat could be made to go further by supplementing it with black-eyed peas and other beans.

Before they set off on the trail or while they were near sources of supplies on the way, the cook would often make up great batches of flavor-rich items, like barbecue sauce, which would keep quite well and would be used to enliven many dishes later. He might also cook up a quantity of scrapple or the like, that could then be fried up for breakfast on subsequent mornings.

SLOPPY JOES

Serves 4–6

1 lb. (450 g) minced beef
1 large onion, chopped
1 celery stalk, chopped
1 green pepper, seeded
    and chopped
4 oz. (115 g) mushrooms, sliced
4 tbsp. tomato ketchup

2 cups (450 ml) tomato juice
salt and pepper
2 tsp. Tabasco or other chili
    sauce (or more if you wish)
2 tbsp. cornstarch
hamburger buns, to serve

1 In a large, dry frying pan, brown the meat well all over, breaking up lumps. Stir in the vegetables and continue to cook until they are tender.

2 Add the ketchup and tomato juice with some seasoning and Tabasco sauce to taste, then mix in the cornstarch. Mix well and cook on a very low heat for at least 2 hours, but the longer the better.

3 Serve hot on hamburger buns. If you want, you can toast the buns before filling them.

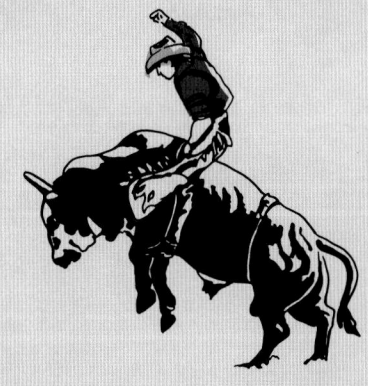

The Cowman's Prayer

Lord, please help me, lend me Thine ear,
The prayer of a troubled cowman to hear.
No doubt my prayer to you may seem strange,
But I want you to bless my cattle range.

Bless the roundups year by year;
Please then don't forget the growing steer.
Water the land with brooks and rills
For my cattle that roam on a thousand hills.

Now O Lord, if you'll be so good,
See that my stock has plenty of food.
Our mountains are peaceful, the prairies serene,
Oh Lord, for the cattle, please keep them green.

Prairie fires, won't you please stop?
Make thunder roll and water to drop,
It frightens me to see the dread smoke,
Unless it is stopped, I'm bound to go dead broke

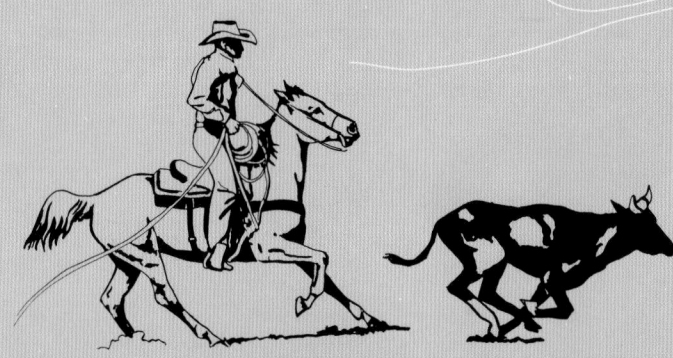
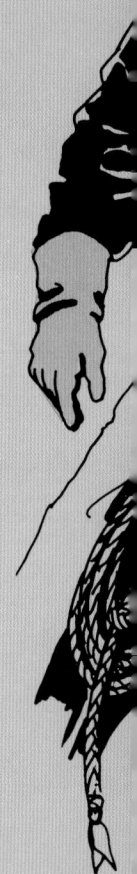

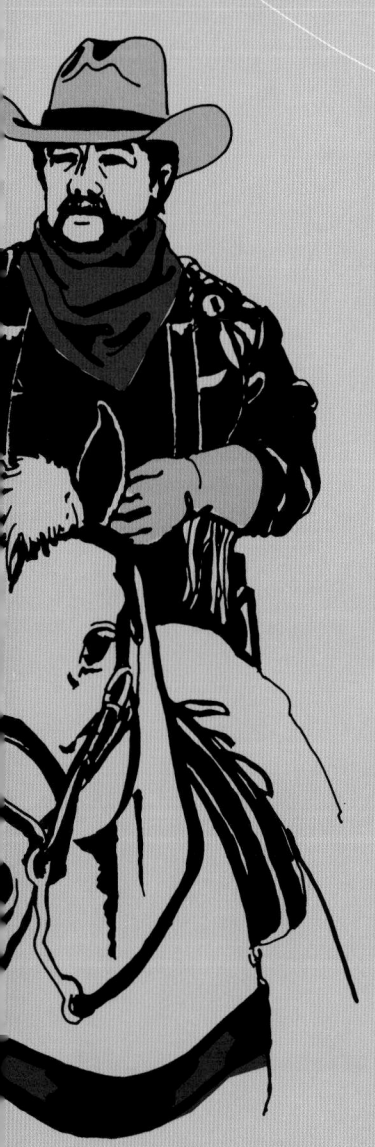

As you, O Lord my fine herds behold,
They represent a sack of pure gold.
I think that at least five cents on the pound
Would be a good price for the beef the year round.

One thing more, and then I'll be through,
Instead of one calf let my cows have two,
I may pray different from all other men
But I've had my say, and now, amen.

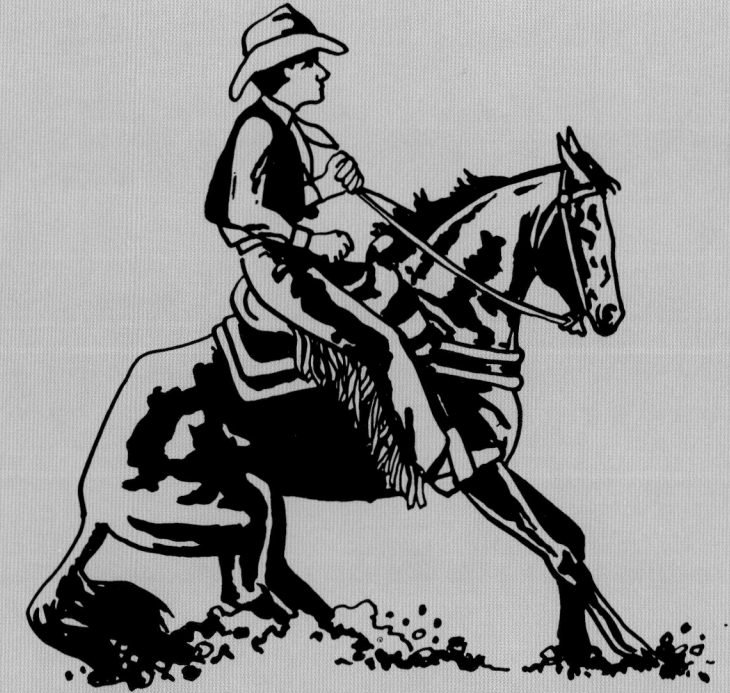

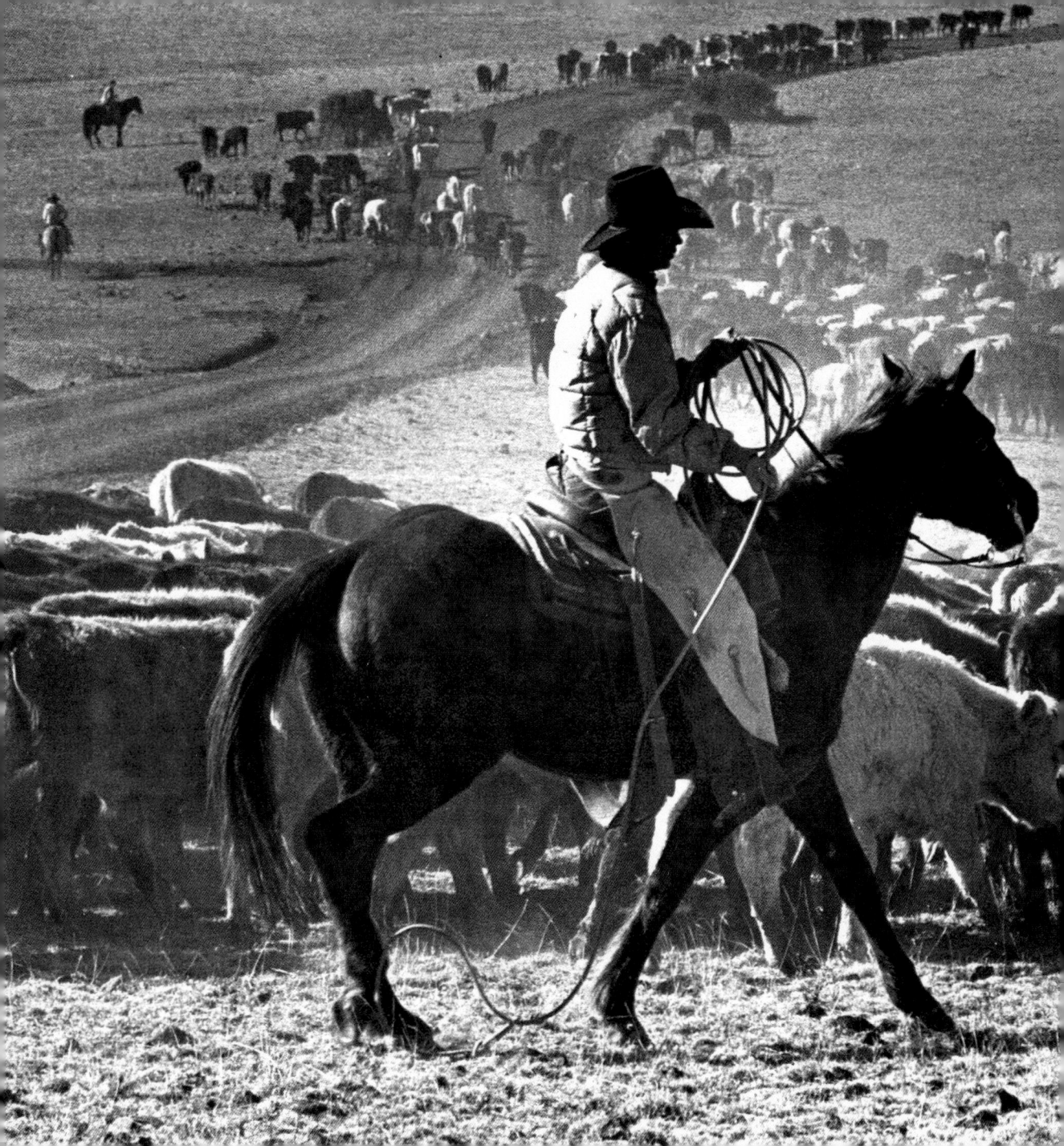

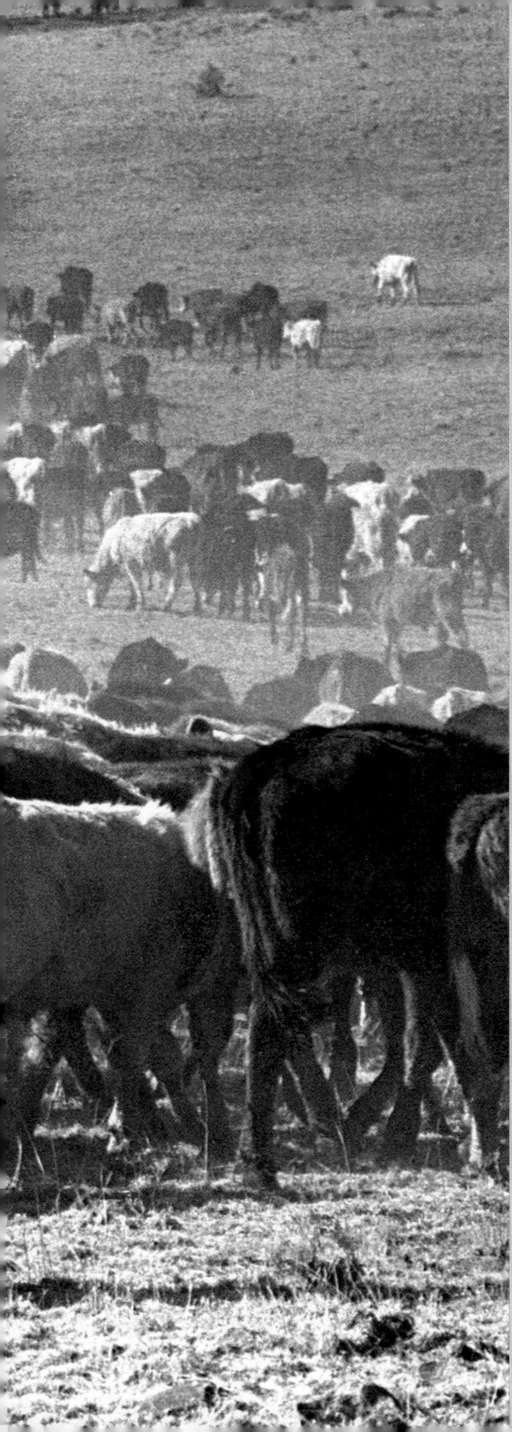

"*I WISH I COULD FIND WORDS TO EXPRESS THE TRUENESS, THE BRAVERY, THE HARDIHOOD, THE SENSE OF HONOR, THE LOYALTY TO THEIR TRUST AND TO EACH OTHER OF THE OLD TRAIL HANDS.*"

Charles Goodnight

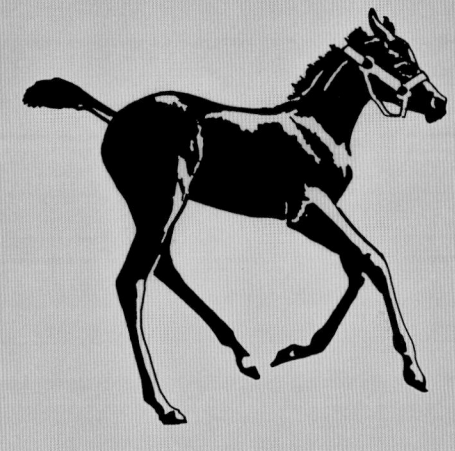

BARBECUE BEEF SHORT RIBS

Serves 4–6

3⅓ lb. (1.5 kg) beef short ribs, cut into serving pieces
salt and pepper
1 onion, sliced
1 carrot, sliced (optional)
2–3 celery stalks, chopped (optional)
12 fl. oz./⅓ cup (350 ml) beer

For the barbecue sauce:
1 tbsp. olive oil
1 onion, chopped
2 garlic cloves, finely chopped

1 small (8 oz./200 g) can diced tomatoes
5 tbsp. tomato paste
3½ fl. oz. (100 ml) beer
1 tbsp. honey or brown sugar
1–2 tbsp. Worcestershire sauce
2 tsp. hot pepper sauce (optional)
1 bay leaf
½ tsp. crushed chili flakes
1 tsp. dried thyme
2 tsp. lemon juice

1 First make the sauce: Heat the oil in a large heavy-duty pot and sauté the onion and garlic until golden, about 3 minutes. Stir in the remaining ingredients. Bring to a boil, lower the heat, and simmer for 30 to 40 minutes.

2 Put the ribs in a large pan and sprinkle with salt and pepper, then scatter over the onion, the carrots, and celery. Pour in the beer and add water to cover the ribs. Bring to a boil, cover the pot, and reduce the heat to low. Simmer until the ribs are tender, about 1 hour.

3 Remove the ribs from the pot and arrange on the barbecue grill. Brush them with the barbecue sauce and cook, turning and basting regularly with the sauce, until the ribs are nicely browned and glazed on all sides, about 20 minutes.

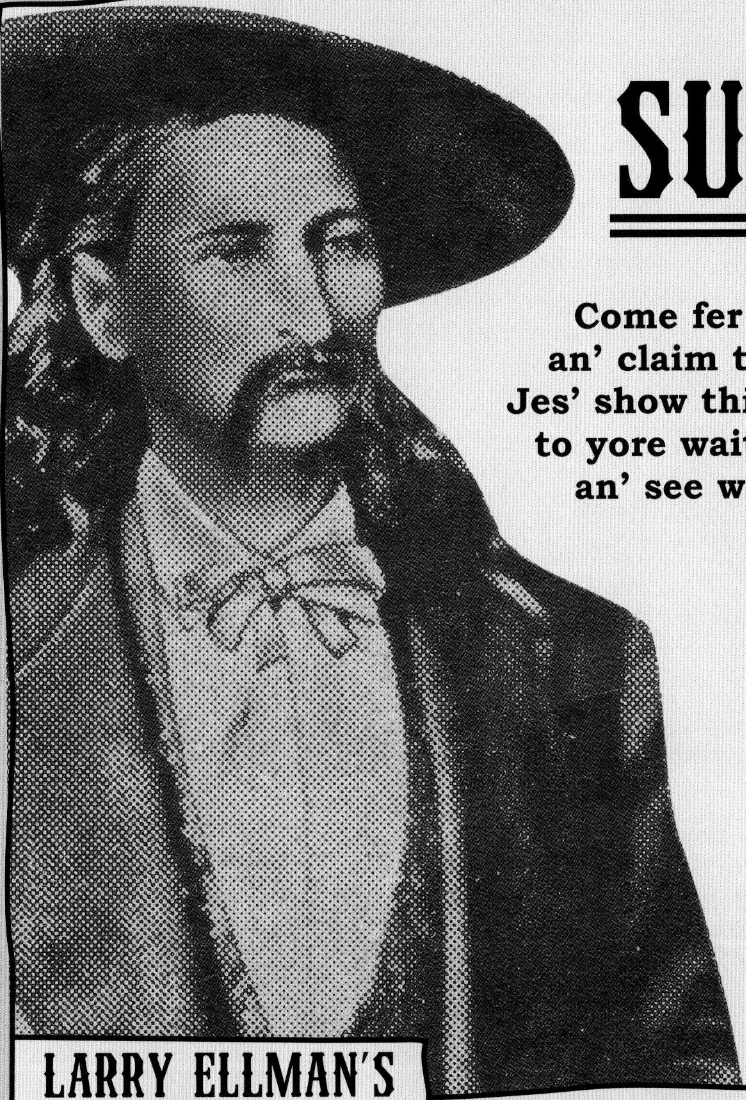

SURPRISE!

Come fer dinner
an' claim the ree-ward!
Jes' show this here ad
to yore waitor
an' see whut happens.

PRAIRIE-SIZE STEAKS
CATTLEMAN'S CUT OF PRIME RIBS

LARRY ELLMAN'S

THE CATTLEMAN

THE ADULT WESTERN RESTAURANT AT 47TH ST. & LEXINGTON AVENUE

Songs and Stampedes

Nighttime could be dangerous on the trail, and the first sign of a storm or a wild animal could send the herd into a furious stampede. Such stampedes could lead to the deaths of several of the cowboys, not to mention countless cows, and would cause many days to be lost in trying to roundup the scattered herd. The cowhands on night watch often sang to keep the cattle calm—"Home on the Range" and "Bury Me Not on the Lone Prairie" were favorites. But just imagine what could happen when the songs didn't work...

"If the cattle started running—you'd hear that low rumbling noise along the ground and the men on herd wouldn't need to come in and tell you, you'd know—then you'd jump for your horse and get out there in the lead, trying to head them and get them into a mill before they scattered to hell and gone. It was riding at a dead run in the dark, with cut banks and prairie dogs holes all around you, not knowing if the next jump would land you in a shallow grave."

Teddy Blue Abbott, cowboy, quoted by Geoffrey C. Ward in THE WEST, AN ILLUSTRATED HISTORY.

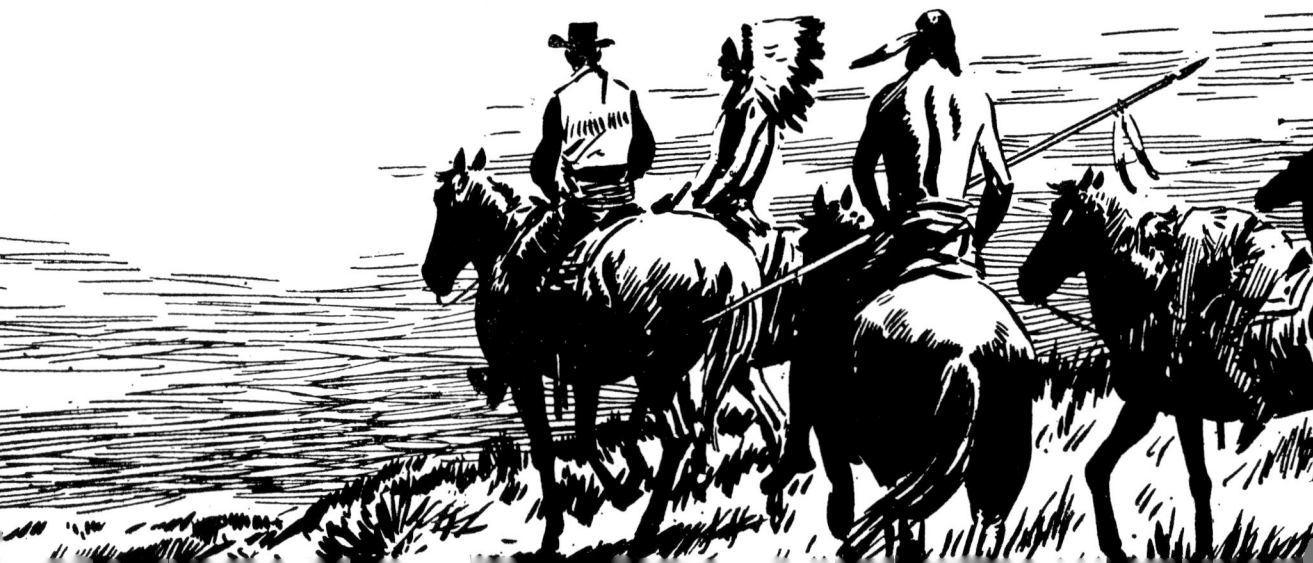

Home On The Range

Oh give me a home, where the buffalo roam,
Where the deer and the antelope play,
Where seldom is heard a discouraging word,
And the skies are not cloudy all day.

Chorus:
Home, home on the range,
Where the deer and the antelope play;
Where seldom is heard a discouraging word,
And the skies are not cloudy all day.

Where the air is so pure, the zephyrs so free,
The breezes so balmy and light,
That I would not exchange my home on the range
For all the cities so bright. **(Chorus)**

The red man was pressed from this part of the West,
He's likely no more to return
To the banks of Red River where seldom if ever
Their flickering campfires burn. **(Chorus)**

How often at night when the heavens are bright
With the light of the glimmering stars,
I have stood there amazed, and asked as I gazed
If their glory exceeds that of ours. **(Chorus)**

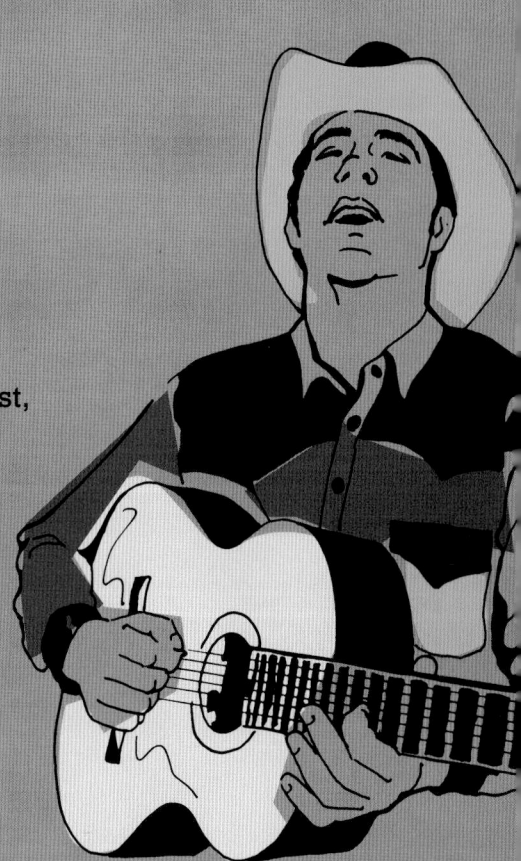

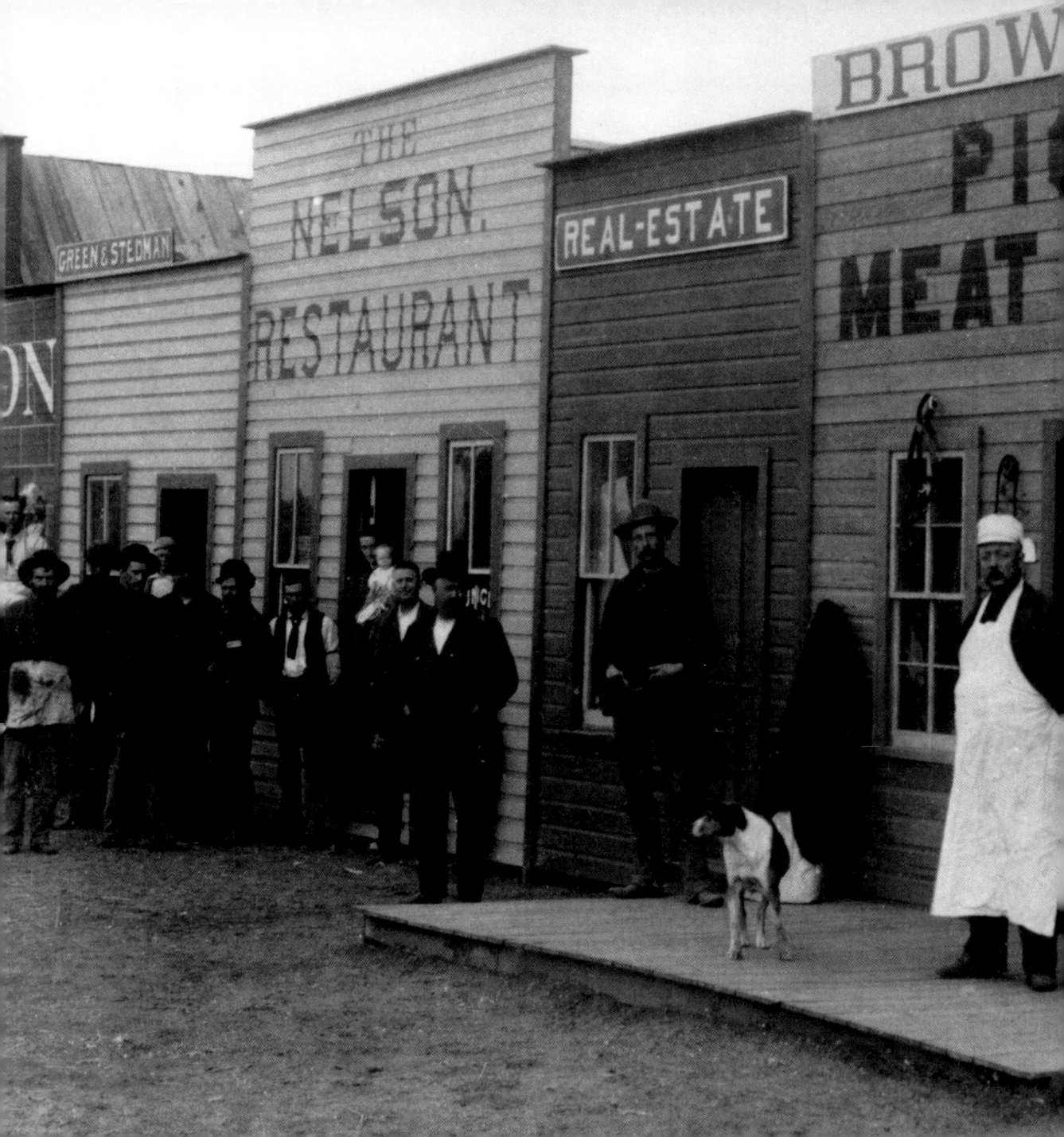

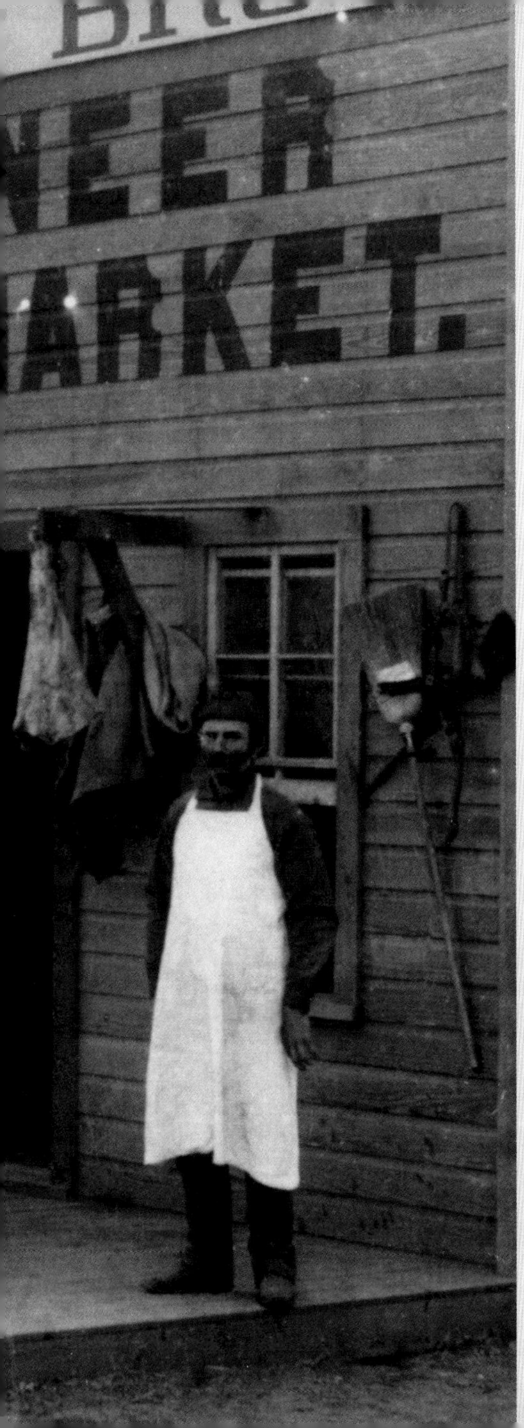

"DODGE IS A ROUGH FRONTIER TOWN, AND IT IS LARGELY POPULATED BY ROUGH PEOPLE, BUT THEY ARE NOT AT ALL VICIOUS. THEY ARE OPEN-HEARTED AND GENEROUS...COWBOYS AND CATTLE DEALERS CONSTITUTE THE BULK OF THE POPULATION."

FROM THE KANSAS COWBOY, DODGE CITY, JULY 12, 1884

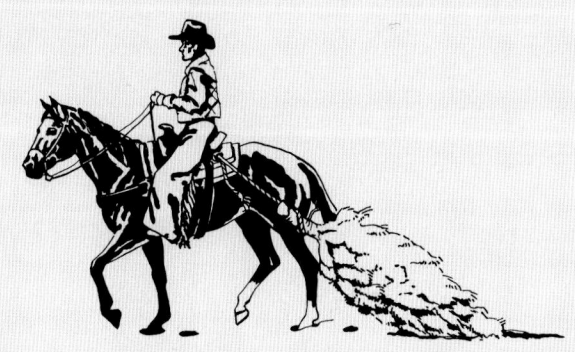

PITCHFORK BEEF FONDUE

Serves 12

oil for deep-frying
12 thick beef steaks (sirloin,
t-bone, or porterhouse)
2–3 garlic cloves (optional) salt
and pepper

To serve:
various mustards
tomato ketchup
steak/barbecue sauces
green salad
biscuits (page 24)

1 Pour the oil into a large, heavy pot set in a very steady position over the fire or on the grill. Rub the steaks with a halved garlic clove if you like and then season them well with salt and pepper. Oil the prongs of 2 to 3 well-scrubbed pitchforks (or 12 long metal skewers) and arrange the steaks on them. (Arrange them so that those to be cooked to the same degree are on the same forks).

2 When a piece of bread dropped into the hot oil browns in 60 seconds, fry the steaks in batches (one fork or 3 to 4 skewers at a time). Cook the steaks for 1 to 2 minutes for rare, 2 to 2½ minutes for medium-rare, and 3 minutes for medium.

3 Carefully remove from the oil. Use tongs to remove the steaks from the prongs, and drain well on crumpled paper towels for 2 or 3 minutes before serving. (This allows the cooked meat to rest and become juicier).

4 Serve with lots of accompaniments, as above.

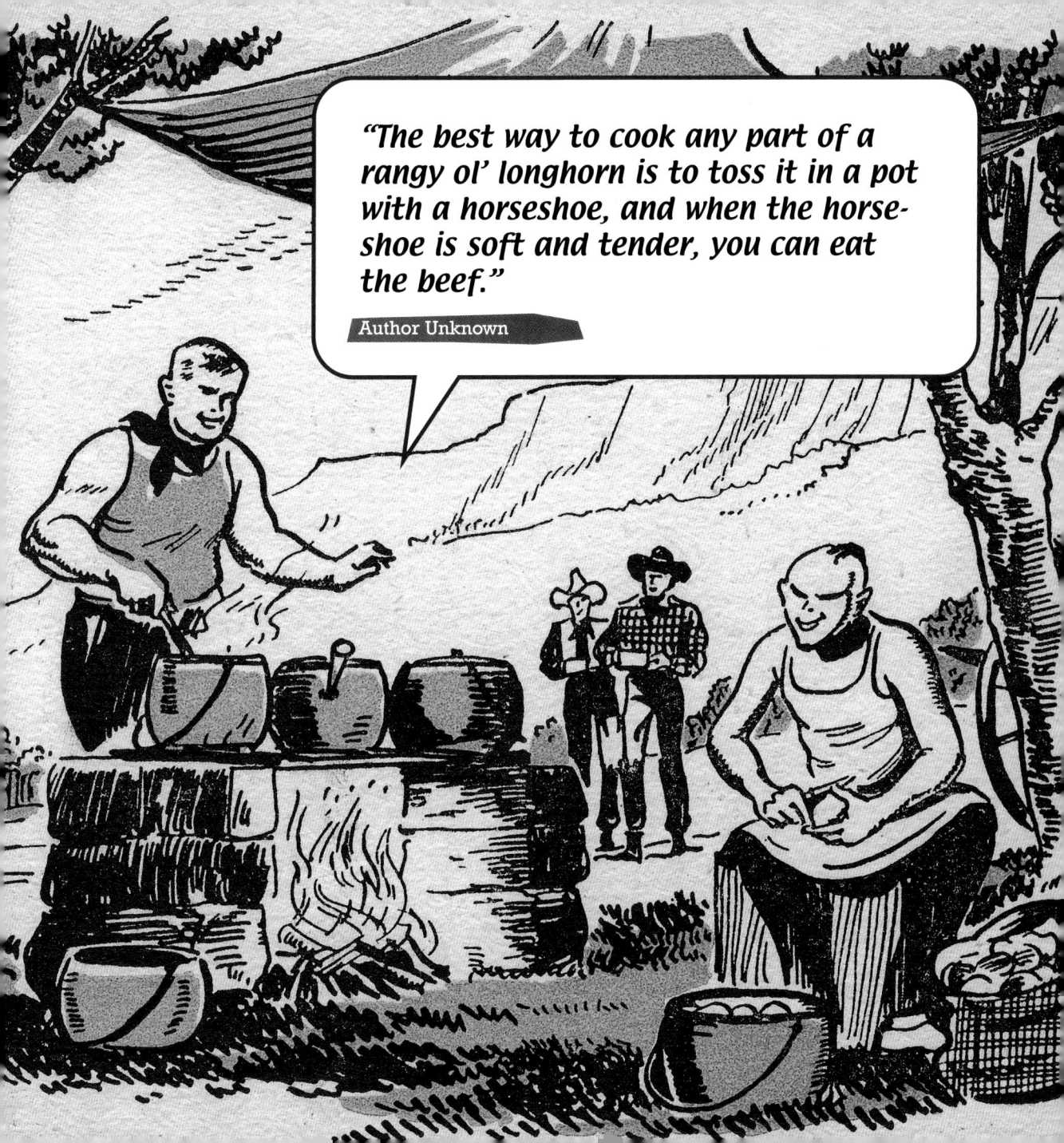

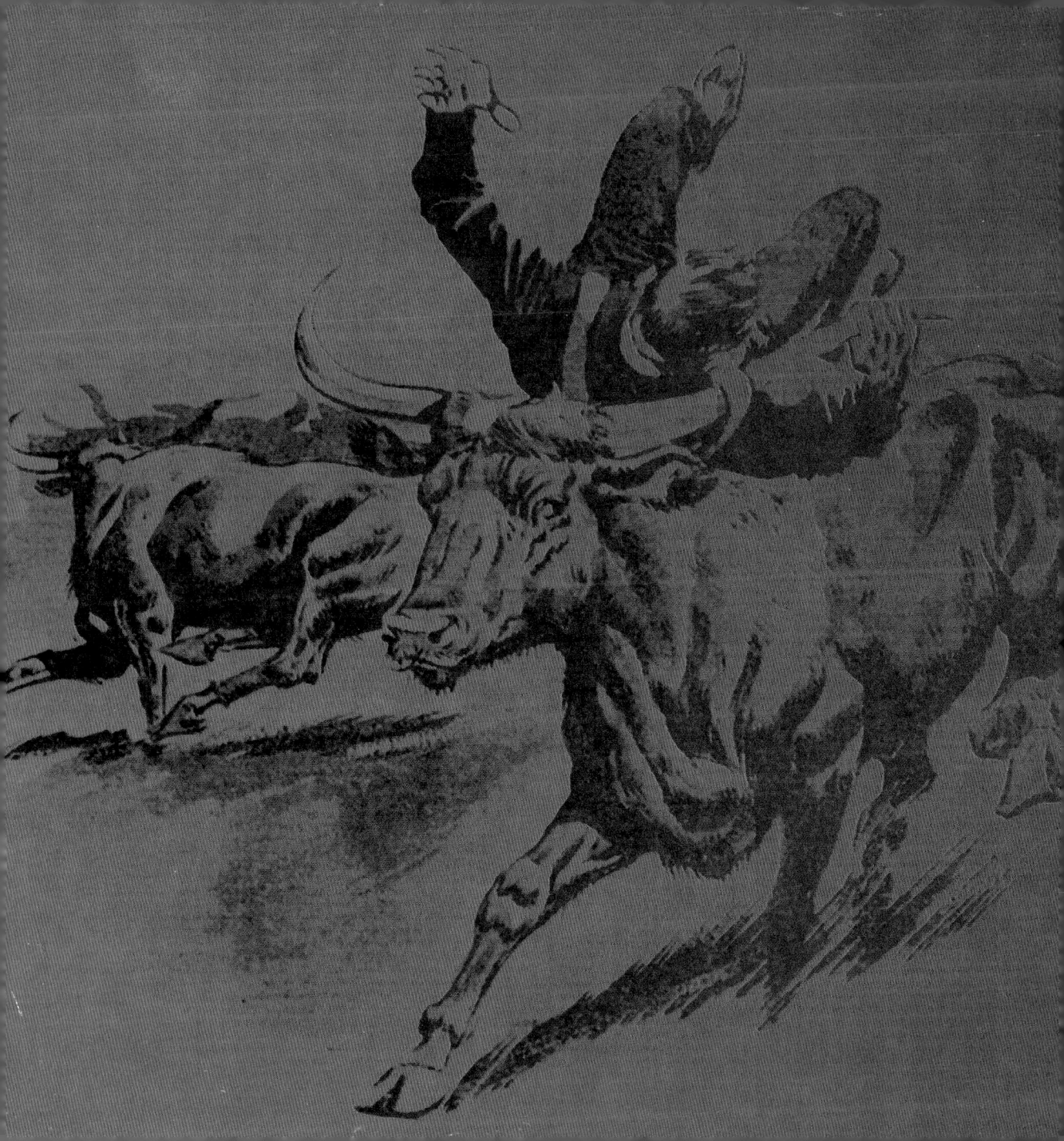

Texas Beef Pot Roast

Serves 6

3½ oz. (100 g) vegetable shortening or lard or 3½ fl. oz. (100 ml) vegetable oil
4–5 lb. (2–2.5 kg) beef pot roast (chuck, shoulder, or rump)
3 oz./½ cup (75 g) flour
salt and pepper
1 onion, peeled and cut into 8 pieces

4 large baking potatoes, peeled and cut into 6–8 pieces
4 carrots, peeled and cut into pieces
2 celery stalks, chopped
2 garlic cloves, thinly sliced
1 bay leaf

1 Heat the vegetable shortening, lard, or oil in a frying pan over a medium heat. Rub the roast with the some of the flour, which has been seasoned with salt and pepper, then brown it on all sides in the hot fat, turning several times.

2 Put the browned roast in a large pot, fat side up. Place the onion, potatoes, carrots, celery, garlic, and bay leaf around the beef and season again with salt and pepper. And enough hot water to cover everything in the pot by about an inch. Cover the pot tightly and cook for about 4 hours, until the meat is tender.

3 Transfer the cooked roast and vegetables to a serving plate and keep warm. Mix the remaining flour with some cold water to make a paste. Gradually whisk the mixture into the pan juices, stirring constantly, until the gravy is smooth and thick, 2 to 3 minutes.

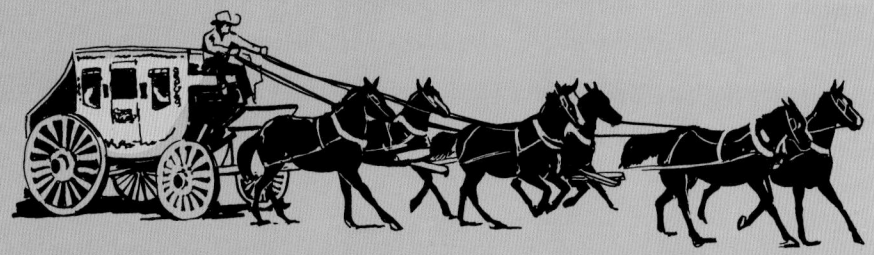

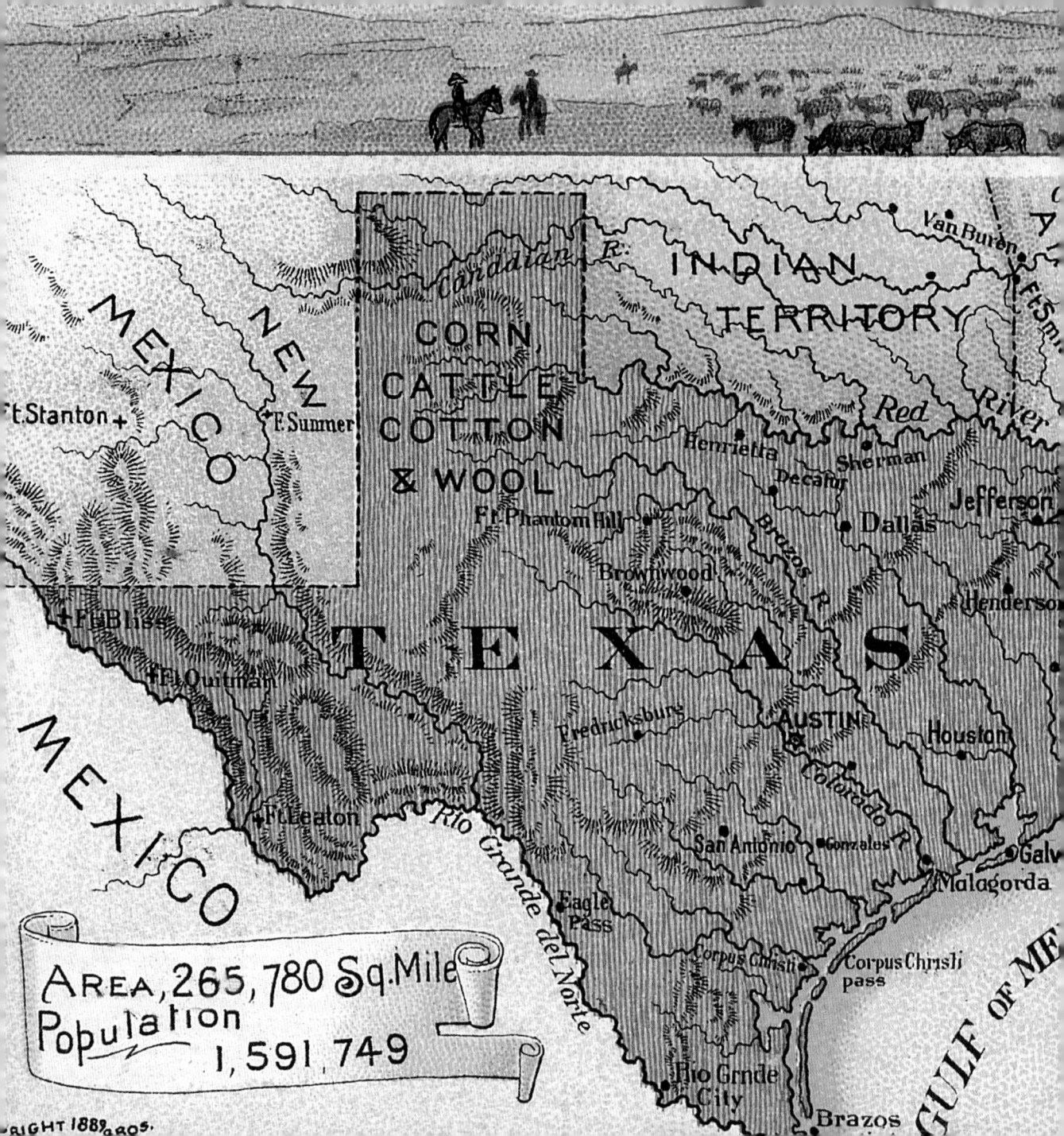

MEXICO

NEW

+Ft.Stanton

F.Summer

Canadian R.

INDIAN

TERRITORY

Van Buren

Ft.Sm

CORN,
CATTLE
COTTON
& WOOL

Red

River

Ft.Phantom Hill

Henrietta

Decatur

Sherman

Jefferson

Brazos

Dallas

Brownwood

Henderson

+Ft.Bliss

T E X A S

+Ft.Quitman

MEXICO

Fredricksburg

AUSTIN

Houston

Colorado

+Ft.Leaton

Rio Grande del Norte

San Antonio

Gonzales

Galv

Malagorda

Eagle
Pass

Corpus Christi

Corpus Christi
pass

AREA, 265,780 Sq.Mile
Population
1,591,749

GULF OF ME

Rio Grnde
City

Brazos

RIGHT 1889 BROS.

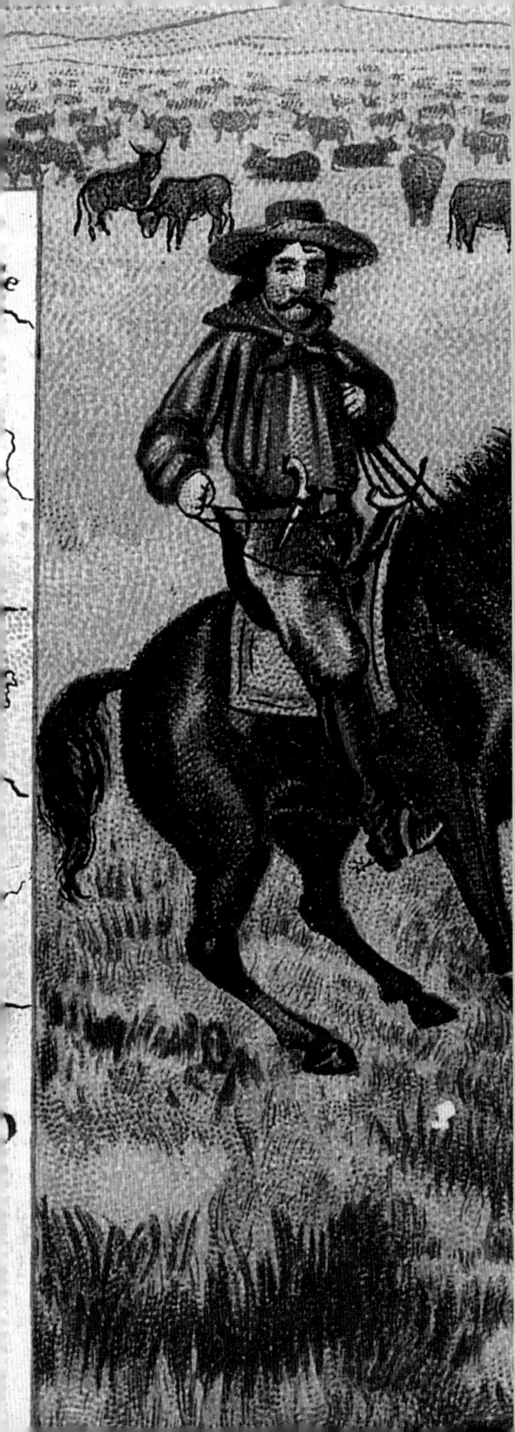

"I MUST SAY AS TO WHAT I HAVE SEEN OF TEXAS, IT IS THE GARDEN SPOT OF THE WORLD, THE BEST LAND AND THE BEST PROSPECTS FOR HEALTH I EVER SAW."

Davy Crockett

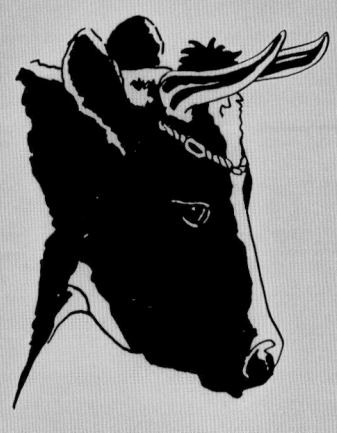

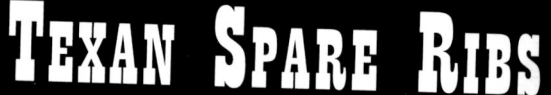

TEXAN SPARE RIBS

Serves 6–8

6½ lb. (3 kg) pork spare ribs, separated

For the marinade:
⅓ cup (75 g) brown sugar
1 tbsp. paprika
1 tsp. salt
1–2 tsp. English mustard powder
1–2 tsp. chili powder
1 tsp. ground cinnamon
2 tbsp. Worcestershire sauce
4 tbsp. white wine vinegar
6 tbsp. tomato paste
juice of 1 lemon
1 small onion, finely chopped

1 First prepare the marinade by mixing together all the ingredients in a saucepan and simmering the mixture over a low heat for 10 to 15 minutes.

2 Arrange the ribs in a single layer on a large sheet of heavy-duty foil with its edges folded up to make a tray. Pour the marinade over the ribs and wrap the foil around them to make a big parcel. Double wrap with another sheet of foil. Refrigerate for at least an hour or until ready to cook.

3 When ready to cook, place the parcel on the side of the fire or barbecue and cook slowly for 1 to 1½ hours. Once in a while, using oven mitts, remove the parcel and give it a quick shake in order to baste the ribs.

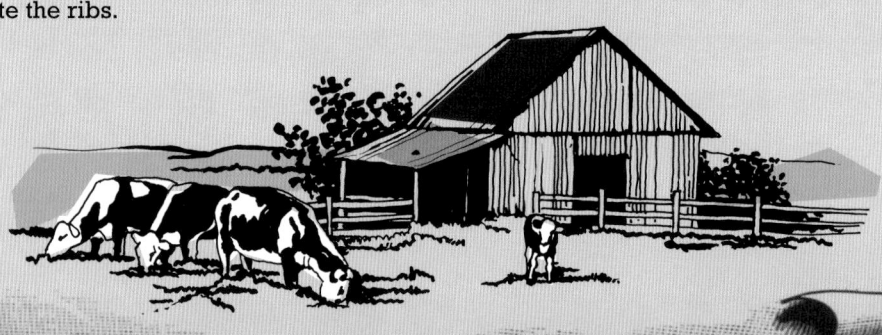

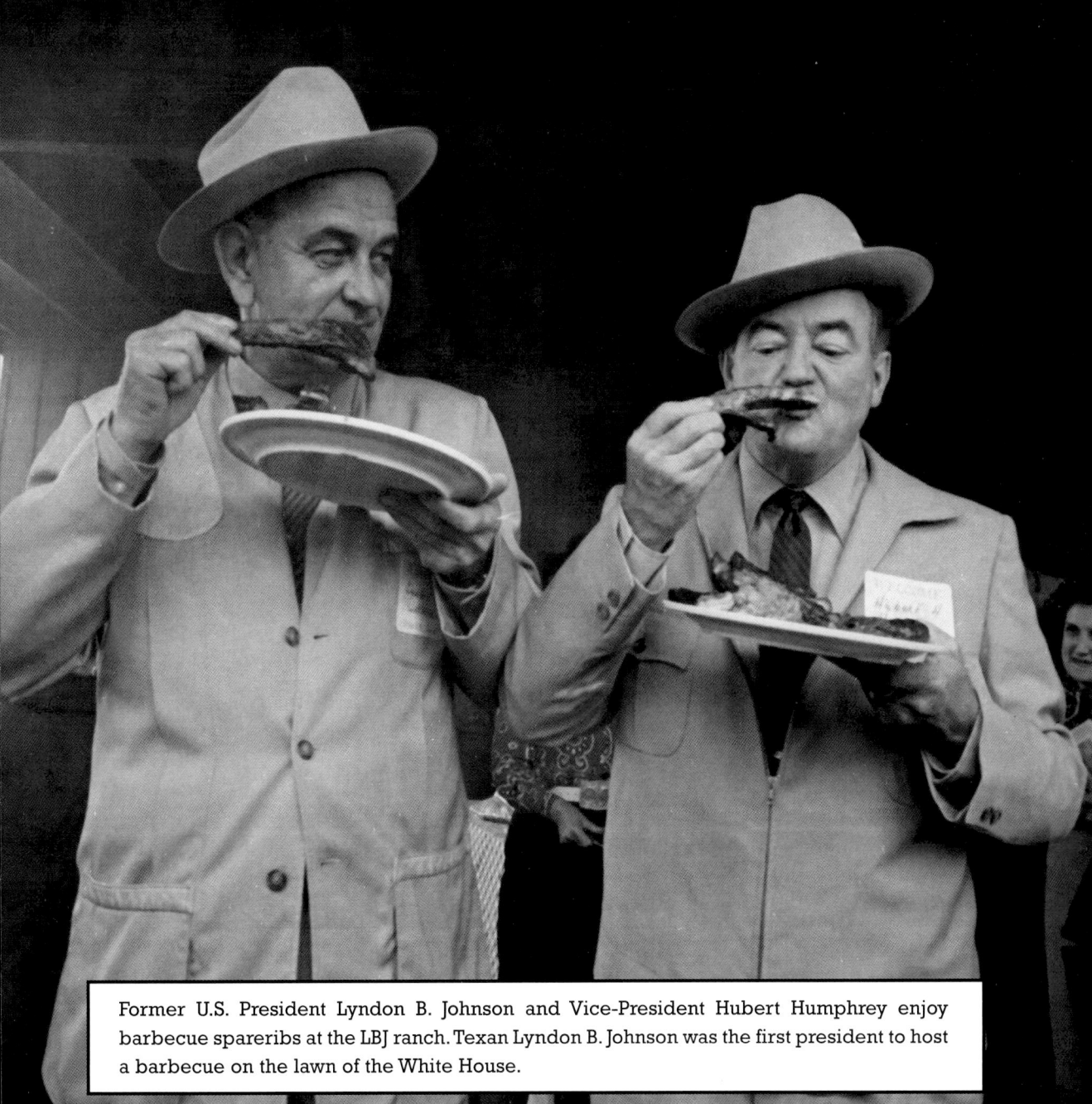

Former U.S. President Lyndon B. Johnson and Vice-President Hubert Humphrey enjoy barbecue spareribs at the LBJ ranch. Texan Lyndon B. Johnson was the first president to host a barbecue on the lawn of the White House.

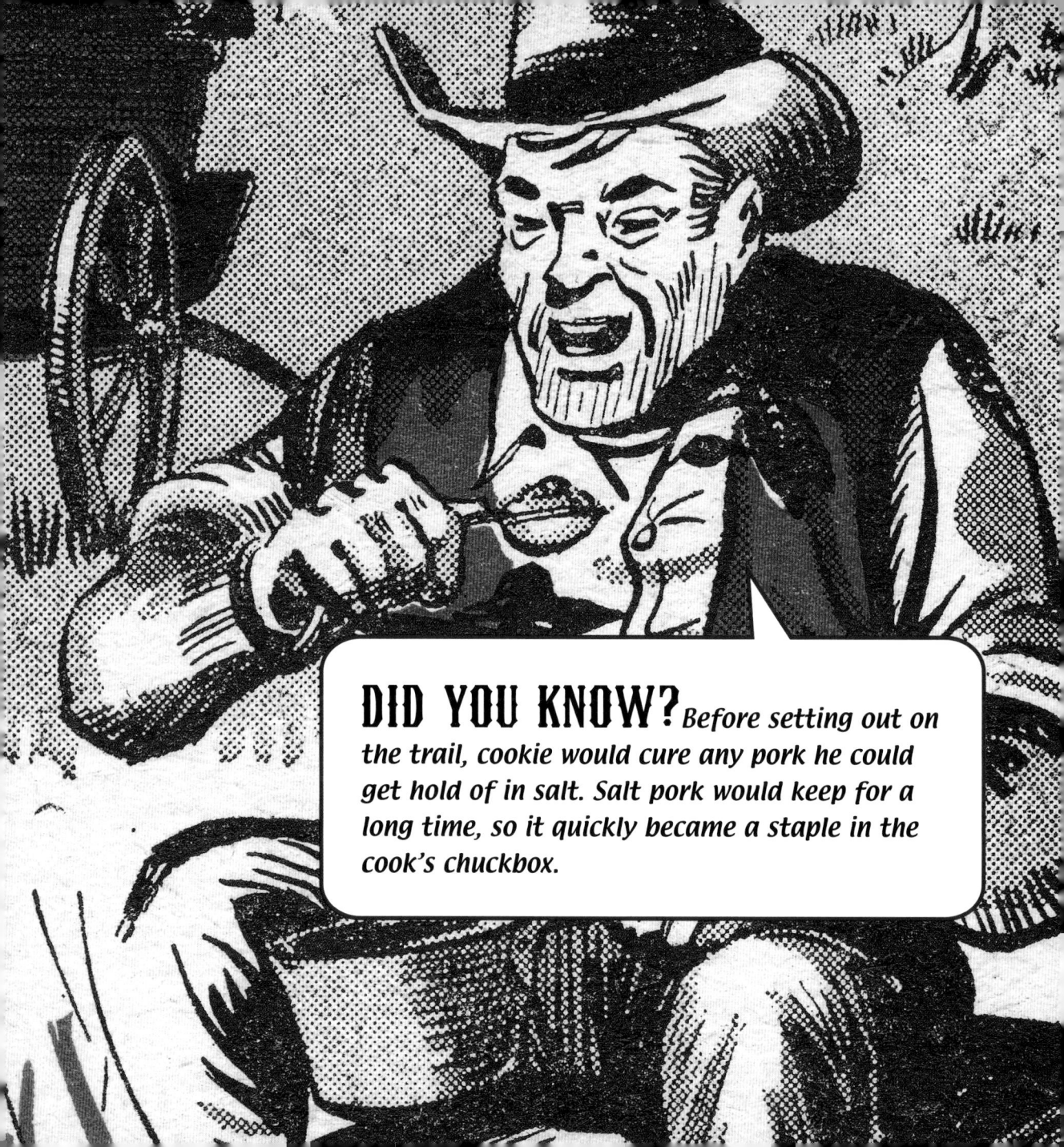

SALT PORK IN MILK GRAVY

Serves 4

1 lb. (450 g) salt pork, thinly sliced
2 cups (450 ml) boiling water
cornmeal or quick-cooking polenta, for dusting

1 small onion, finely chopped
2 tbsp. flour
8 fl. oz./1 cup (225 ml) milk

1 Dip the slices of salt pork in the boiling water, drain, and then dip in the cornmeal or polenta on both sides. Dip the slices of salt pork in the boiling water, drain and then dip in the cornmeal or polenta on both sides.

2 Brown the pork slices in a large frying pan, turning them often, until cooked through (you may have to do this in batches). Remove the pork from the pan and set aside.

3 Pour off all but a few spoonfuls of the fat from the pan and cook the onion until browned. Sprinkle in the flour and cook, stirring, until the flour is well blended. Gradually add the milk, stirring all the time, and bring to a simmer. Cook, stirring continuously, until the gravy is thick and smooth.

4 Serve with biscuits (page 24) or corn bread (page 112).

You can spice this up a bit by adding some dried chili flakes or Tabasco sauce; a sprinkling of dried sage is also good.

PORK SCRAPPLE

2 lb. (900 g) pork neck (or other bony cut of pork with lots of flavor)
2 onions
6 black peppercorns
1 small bay leaf (optional)
1 cup cornmeal or quick-cooking polenta

1 tsp. salt
½ tsp. dried thyme or sage
freshly grated nutmeg
a little cayenne pepper
bacon drippings or lard, for frying
7½ cups (1½ liters) cold water

1 Put the pork in a pot with 1 of the onions, sliced, the peppercorns, the bay leaf if using, and 7 cups (1½ liters) cold water. Bring to a boil and then simmer gently until the meat is falling from the bone. Strain off the liquid. (There should be about 4 cups; if not, make up the difference with water.) Bring back to a simmer in a large heavy pan.

2 Make a paste by mixing the cornmeal or polenta with ½ cup (125 ml) cold water and the salt in a bowl. Slowly stir this mixture into the boiling stock and continue to stir over a moderate heat for a few minutes. Cover tightly and cook very slowly for 25 to 30 minutes, stirring frequently.

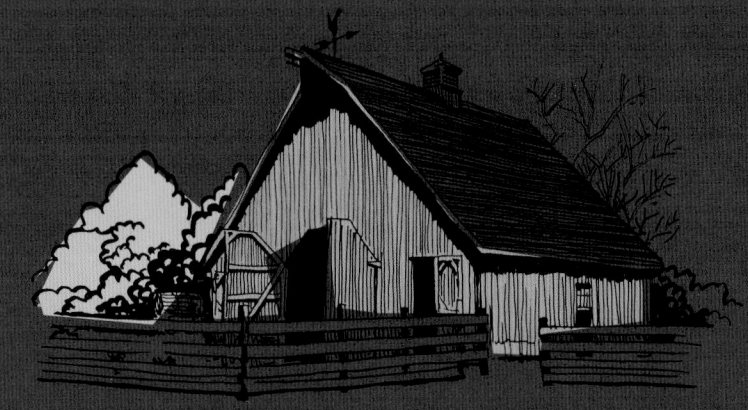

3 Remove all the meat from the pork bones and chop finely. Add to the cooked paste and season with more salt, if necessary. Add the remaining onion, grated, the thyme or sage, and nutmeg and cayenne to taste. Stir well.

4 Rinse out a bread pan with cold water and pour the mixture into it. Let it sit at room temperature until cold and firm.

5 To serve, cut into slices and fry the slices slowly in bacon drippings or lard.

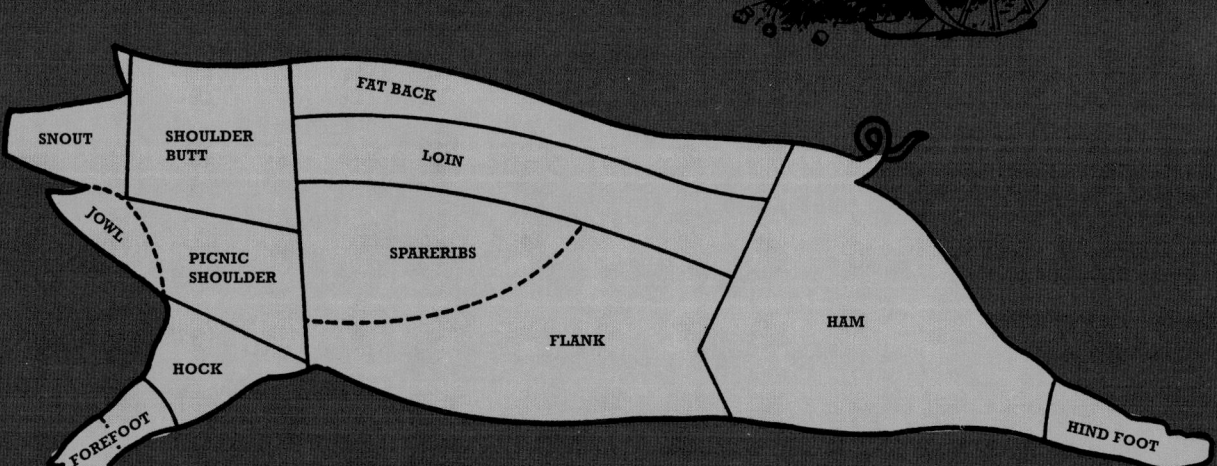

FINGER LICKIN' BARBECUE CHICKEN

Serves 4

1 chicken or 12 chicken pieces, preferably free-range or corn-fed
1 quantity barbecue sauce (page 74)

For the dry marinade:
1 tsp. salt
1 tsp. pepper
½ tsp. cayenne
2 garlic cloves, crushed
1 tsp. mustard powder

1 If using a whole chicken, cut it into pieces, separating the legs into thighs and drumsticks and cutting each side of the breast into 3. With the wings, this gives you 12 pieces. Rinse the pieces and pat dry.

2 Make the dry marinade by mixing all the ingredients. Rub this mixture all over the pieces of chicken. Refrigerate for an hour or so, while getting the barbecue coals or fire hot.

3 Cook the chicken pieces for 20 to 25 minutes, turning once or twice and basting regularly with the barbecue sauce until nicely glazed and the juices run clear when pierced in the thickest parts.

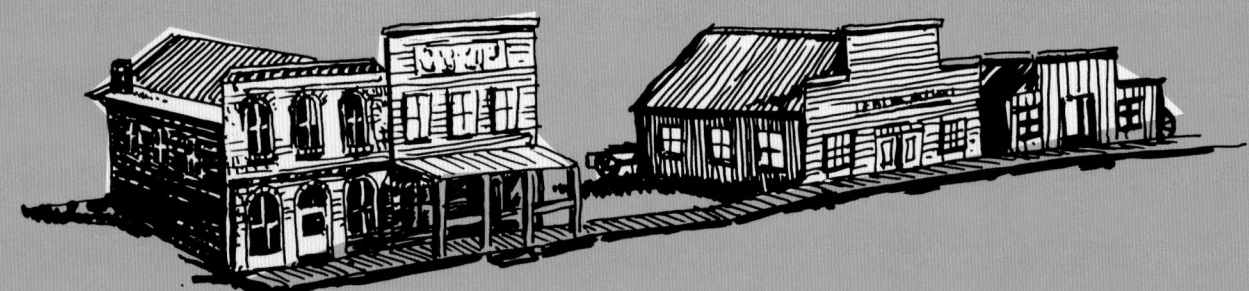

WESTERN FRIED CHICKEN

Serves 4

1 chicken or 12 chicken pieces, preferably free-range or corn-fed
2 eggs
6 oz./¾ cup (150 g) flour
salt and pepper
cayenne pepper

8–12 oz./1–1½ cups (225–350 g) butter
8–12 oz./1–1½ cups (225–350 g) lard or vegetable shortening or
8–12 fl. oz./1–1½ cups (225–350 ml) vegetable oil

1 If using a whole chicken, cut it into pieces, separating the legs into thighs and drumsticks and cutting each side of the breast into 3. With the wings, this gives you 12 pieces. Rinse the pieces and pat dry.

2 In a shallow bowl, beat the eggs with 2 tablespoons of water. In another similar bowl, mix the flour and the seasonings. Dip each piece of chicken first in the egg and then in the seasoned flour, shaking off excess in each case. Repeat the process to give each piece a second coating. Put to one side.

3 Melt the butter and lard or shortening in a large heavy frying pan or add the oil and heat to medium-high (a piece of stale bread will brown in 60 seconds). Fry the chicken pieces, skin side down, in a single, well-spaced layer (you may need to do this in batches), turning them frequently until a good golden color all over, 20 to 30 minutes.

4 Drain on paper towel before serving.

For even more flavor and juiciness, marinate the chicken pieces first for about an hour in milk that has been seasoned with a good dash of Tabasco sauce.

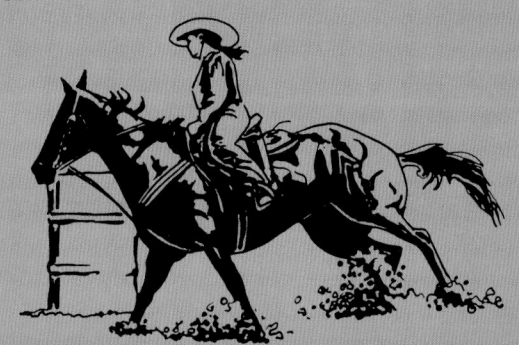

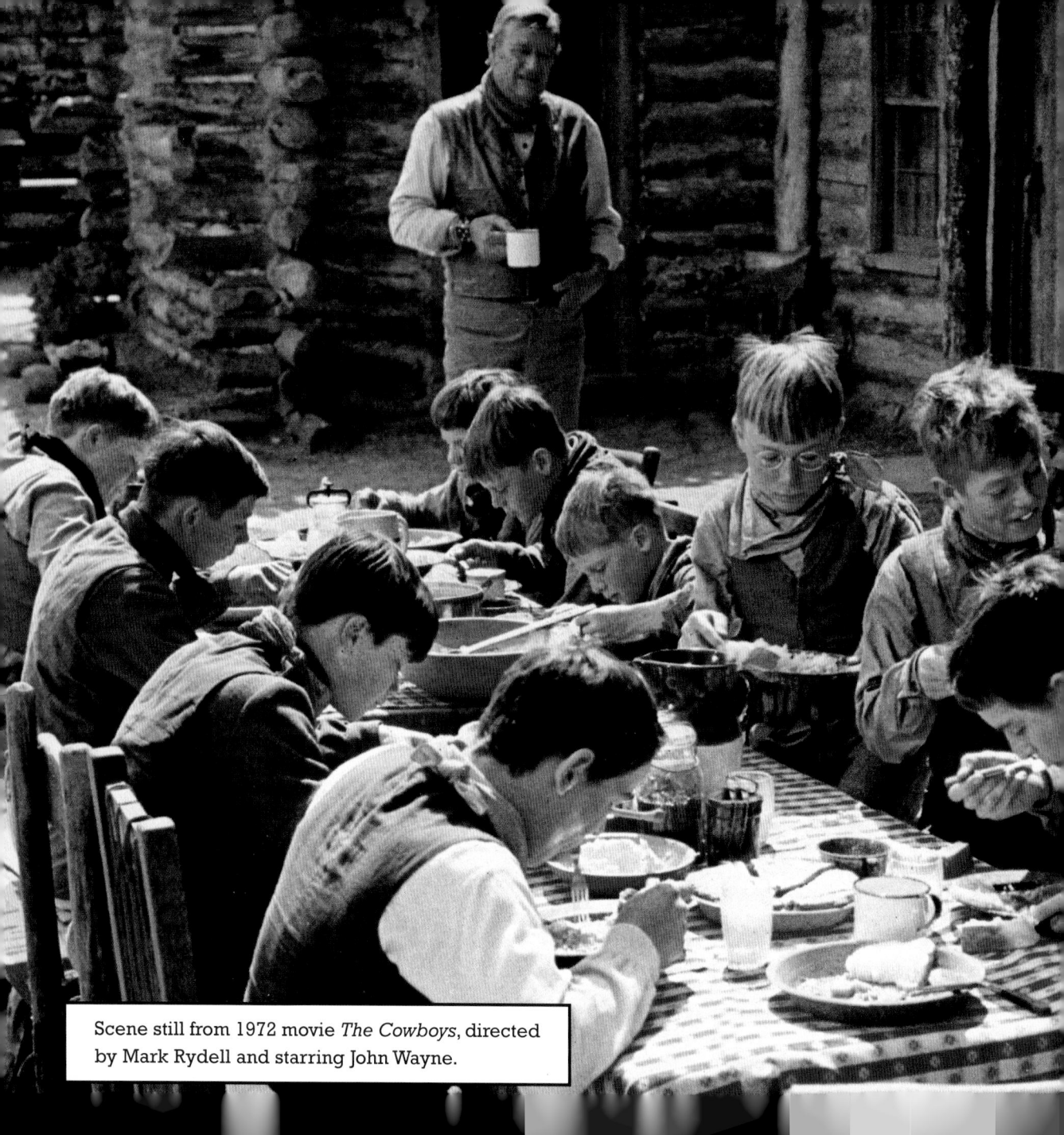

Scene still from 1972 movie *The Cowboys*, directed by Mark Rydell and starring John Wayne.

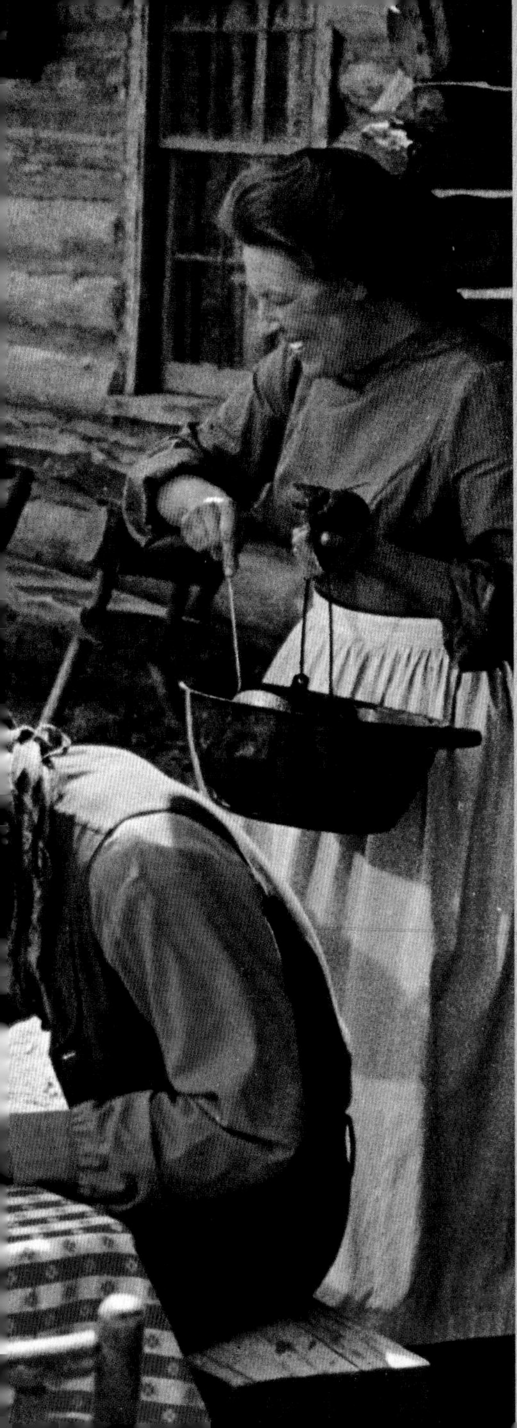

> ## "*GO WEST, YOUNG MAN, AND GROW UP WITH THE COUNTRY.*"
>
> Horace Greeley

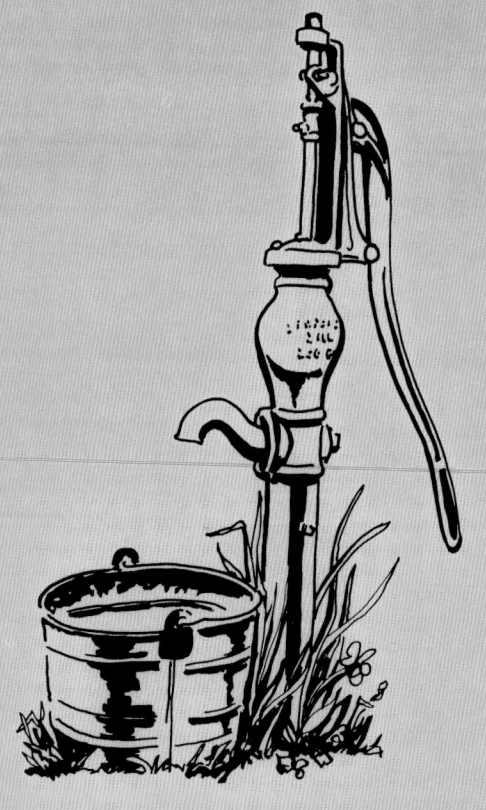

TURKEY STEW
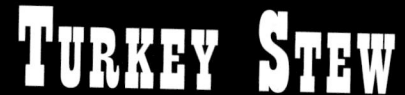
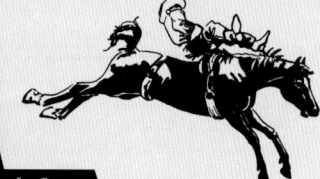

Serves 4–6

3–5 lb. (1.35–2.25 kg) turkey pieces	2 tbsp. oil
3 onions	2 tbsp. flour
3 carrots	6 tbsp. tomato paste
2 celery stalks	14.5 oz. (400 g) can diced tomatoes
1 garlic bulb	1 tsp. dried oregano
salt	½ tsp. ground cumin
a few black peppercorns	4 potatoes

1 A day ahead, put the turkey in a large pan, add water to cover and add 2 of the onions, cut in half, 2 of the carrots, and the celery stalks, coarsely chopped, and all but 2 of the cloves from the head of garlic. Season with salt to taste and add the black peppercorns. Bring to a boil, reduce the heat, and simmer very gently for 3 hours.

2 Remove the turkey from the liquid, remove the meat from the bones, cut into bite-sized pieces, and refrigerate overnight. Return the bones to the pan and simmer for 1 hour more, adding more water if required to make a rich broth. Strain and chill overnight.

3 The next day, skim off any fat from the stock. Heat the oil in a large frying pan. Chop the reserved onion and cook in the oil until translucent. Stir in the flour, tomato paste, diced tomatoes, reserved garlic, finely chopped, the oregano, cumin, and 3 cups (700 ml) of the stock. Add the potatoes and remaining carrot, both diced, and cook until these are tender, about 20 minutes.

4 Stir in the turkey and simmer for a few minutes to warm through before serving.

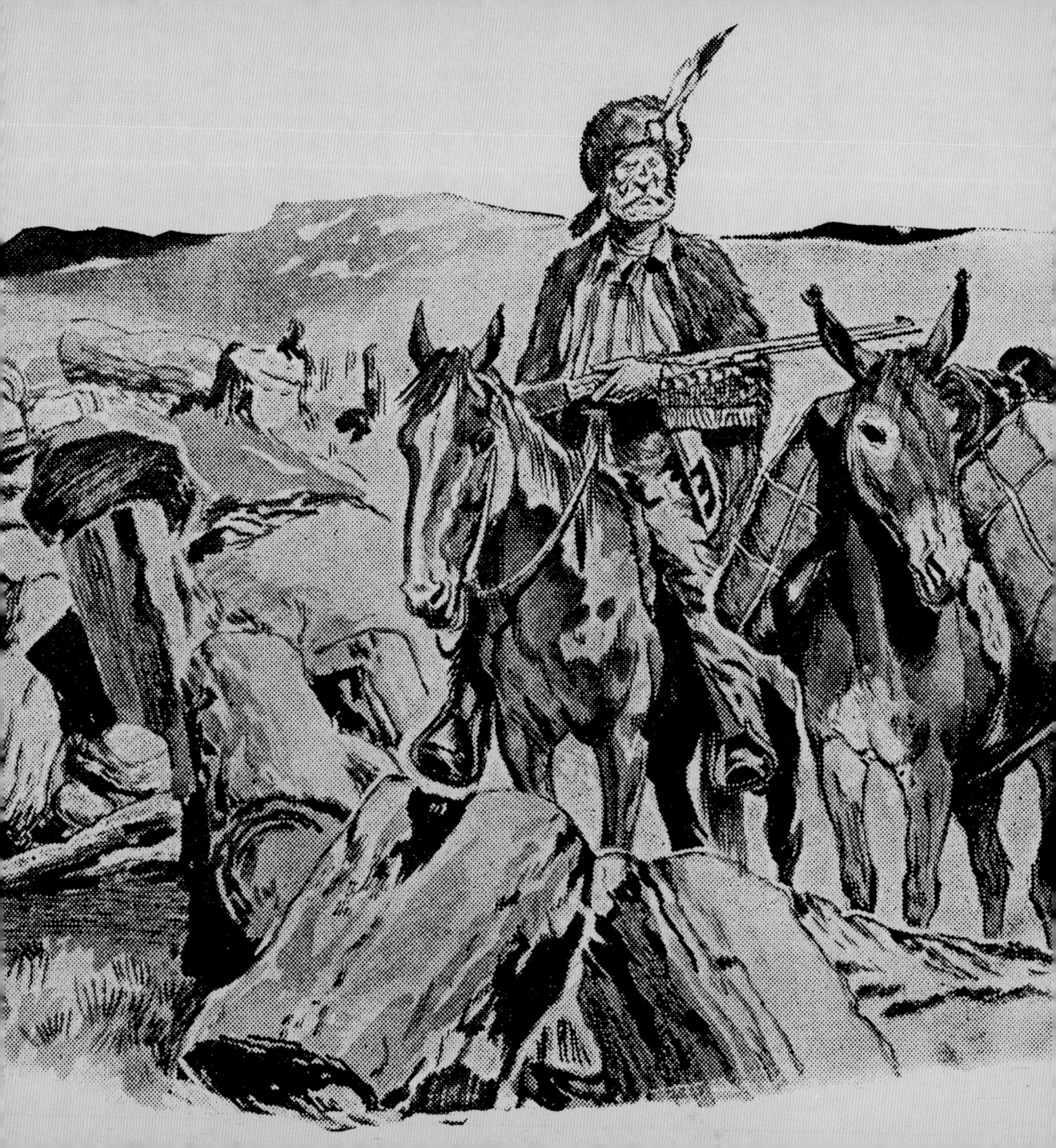

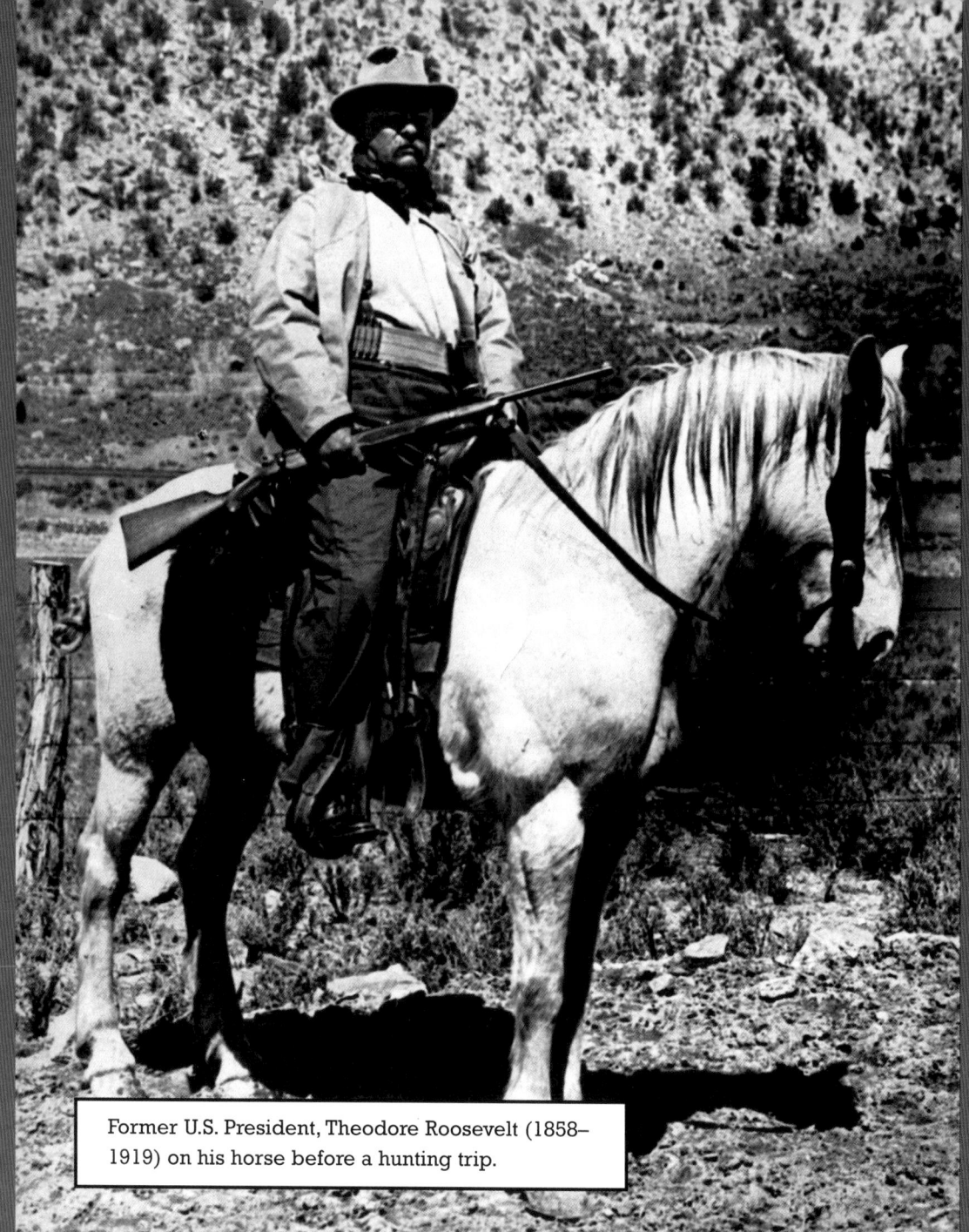

Former U.S. President, Theodore Roosevelt (1858–1919) on his horse before a hunting trip.

Hunting

On the trail, and especially on the cattle ranches, the cowboys sometimes depended on their own hunting skills for food, and a decent cook could work wonders with whatever was caught. A capable hunter was a prized member of the team, and returning with an antelope or a handful of prairie chickens made a cowhand very popular with his companions. Theodore Roosevelt was one such hand during his days on the Dakota ranches, and he recognized the importance of patience and determination above all else when hunting.

"In the old days in the ranch country we depended upon game for fresh meat. … Getting meat for the ranch usually devolved upon me. I almost always carried a rifle when I rode, either in a scabbard under my thigh, or across the pommel. Often I would pick up a deer or antelope while about my regular work, when visiting a line camp or riding after the cattle. At other times I would make a day's trip after them. In the fall we sometimes took a wagon and made a week's hunt, returning with eight or ten deer carcasses, and perhaps an elk or a mountain sheep as well. I never became more than a fair hunter, and at times I had most exasperating experiences, either failing to see game which I ought to have seen, or committing some blunder in the stalk, or failing to kill when I fired. Looking back, I am inclined to say that if I had any good quality as a hunter it was that of perseverance. "It is dogged that does it" in hunting as in many other things."

Theodore Roosevelt, 1913, FROM AN AUTOBIOGRAPHY; "IV: IN COWBOY LAND"

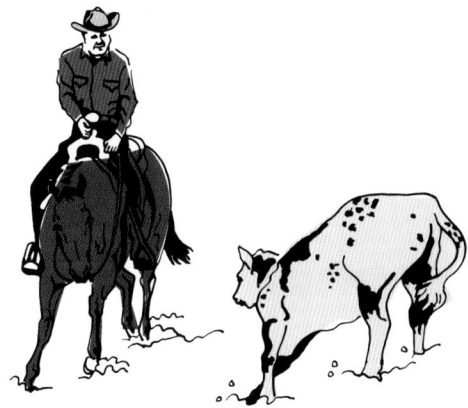

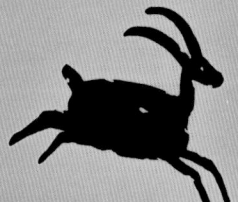
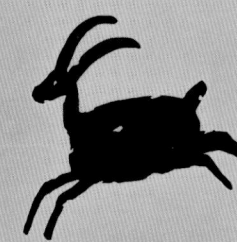

VENISON STEW

Serves 8-10

4½ lb. (2 kg) venison, cut into bite-sized pieces
5–6 onions, quartered
5–6 celery stalks, chopped
salt and pepper
cayenne pepper

9 cups (2 liters) red wine or beer
3 tsp. red wine vinegar or cider vinegar
vegetable oil
5 tbsp. flour
3 cups (700 ml) beef stock or water

1 Several days ahead: In a large mixing bowl, combine the venison pieces with the onions, celery, and salt, pepper, and cayenne to taste. Pour in the wine or beer and the vinegar. Cover, and let marinate in the refrigerator, if possible, or a good cold place, for 2 to 3 days, turning everything 2 or 3 times a day.

2 Drain off the marinade liquid and put the meat and vegetables in separate bowls. Pat the venison dry and brown thoroughly in a little oil in a large heavy-duty pot, in batches if necessary. Remove and set aside.

3 Once all the venison is browned, stir-fry the vegetables for a few minutes in a little more hot oil. Remove from the pan and set aside with the meat.

4 Add 3 tablespoons oil to the pan and stir in the flour to make a roux. Cook gently, stirring, until the flour is dark golden and smells nutty. Gradually stir in the reserved marinade liquid. Add the stock or water, and bring to a boil, stirring continuously.

5 Return the venison and vegetables to the pan and bring to a boil again. Cover tightly and cook at a good simmer for about 1½ hours.

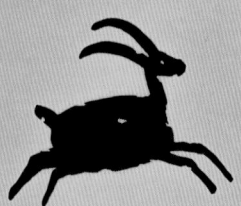
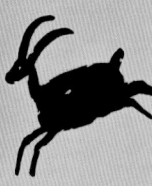

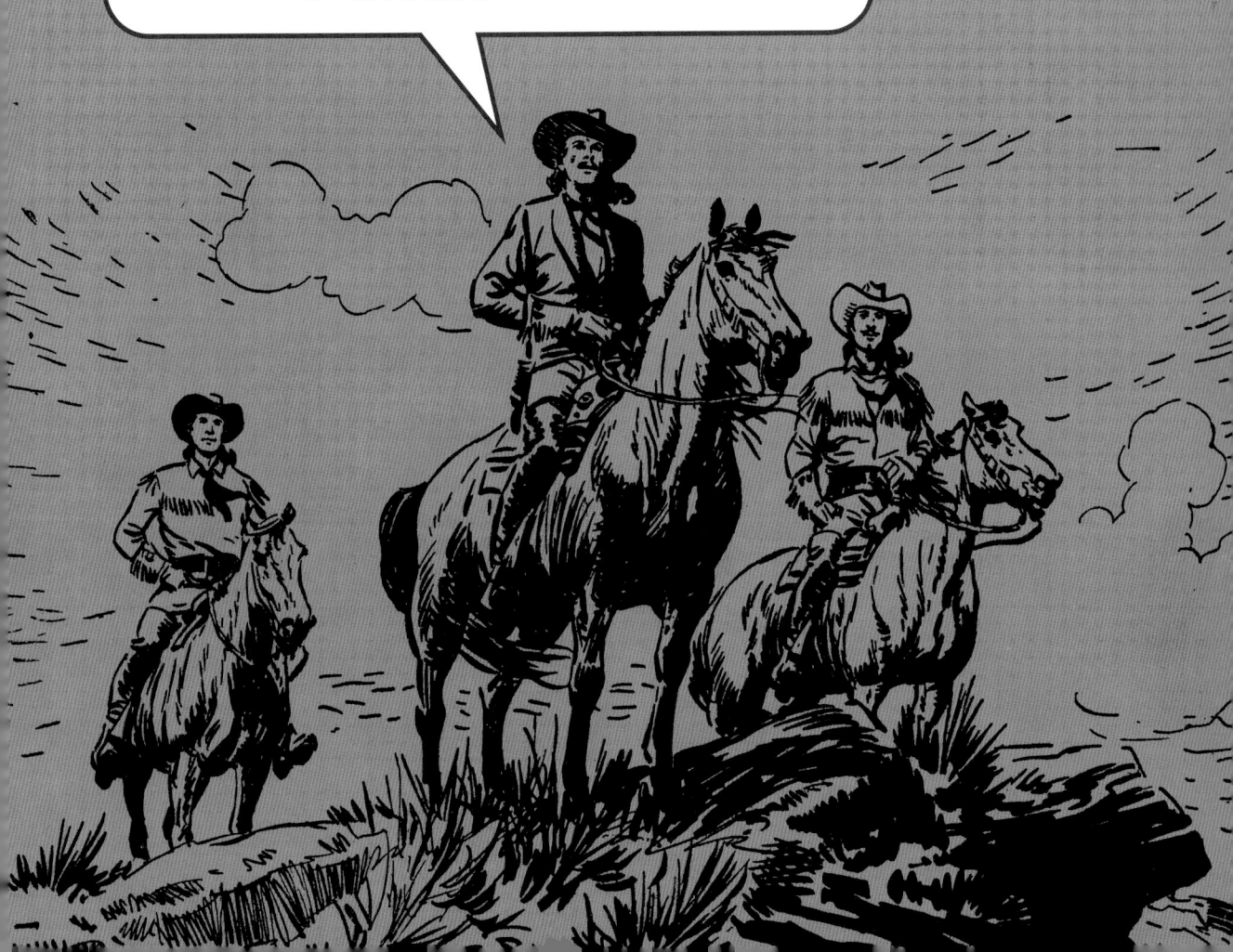

RABBIT CHILI

Serves 4

2 tbsp. oil
2 lb. (900 g) rabbit pieces
4 garlic cloves, crushed
8 fl. oz./1 cup (225 ml) hot water or chicken stock
6 tbsp. tomato paste

14.5 oz. (400 g) can diced tomatoes
2 tsp. chili powder, or 2 chopped fresh chilies, or more to taste
12 oz. (350 g) dried kidney beans
salt and pepper
2 tbsp. grated cheddar cheese

1 Heat the oil in a large heavy-duty pot, add the rabbit and garlic, and brown the rabbit pieces all over.

2 Add the hot water or stock, tomatoes, tomato paste, diced tomatoes, chili, and beans, and season to taste with pepper but not salt. Bring to a boil, lower the heat, and simmer gently for 2 hours.

3 Season to taste with salt. Sprinkle with the cheese just before serving.

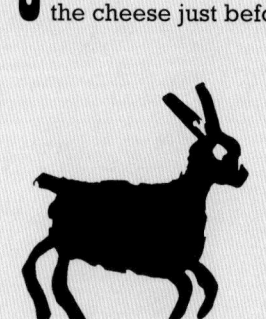

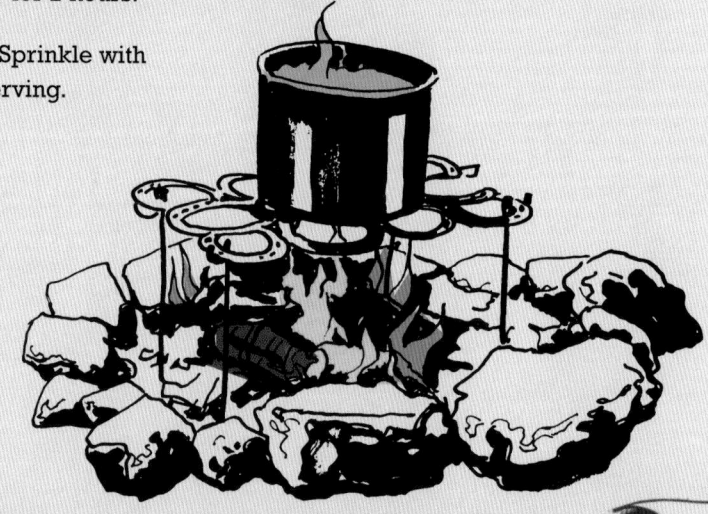

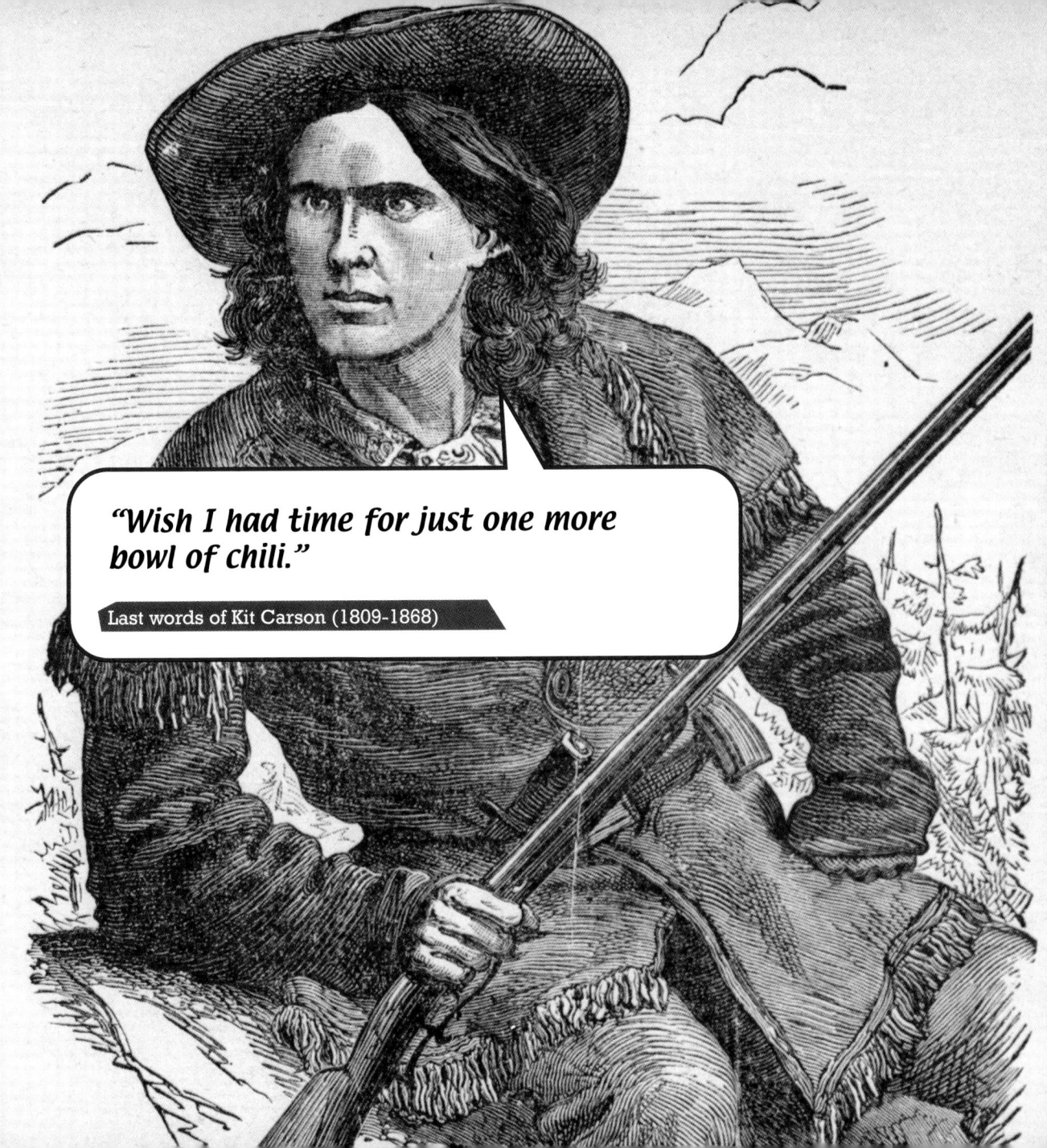

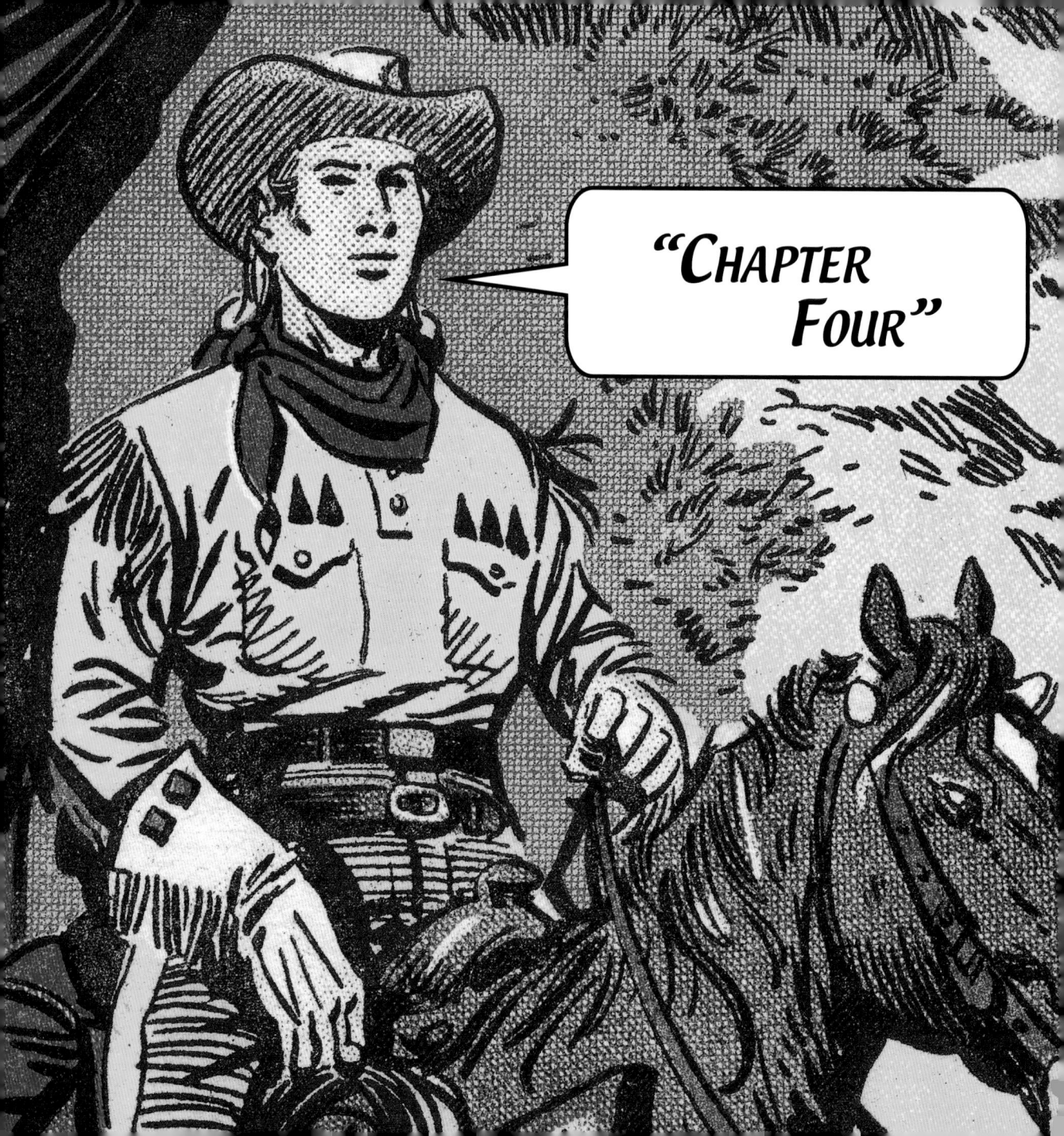

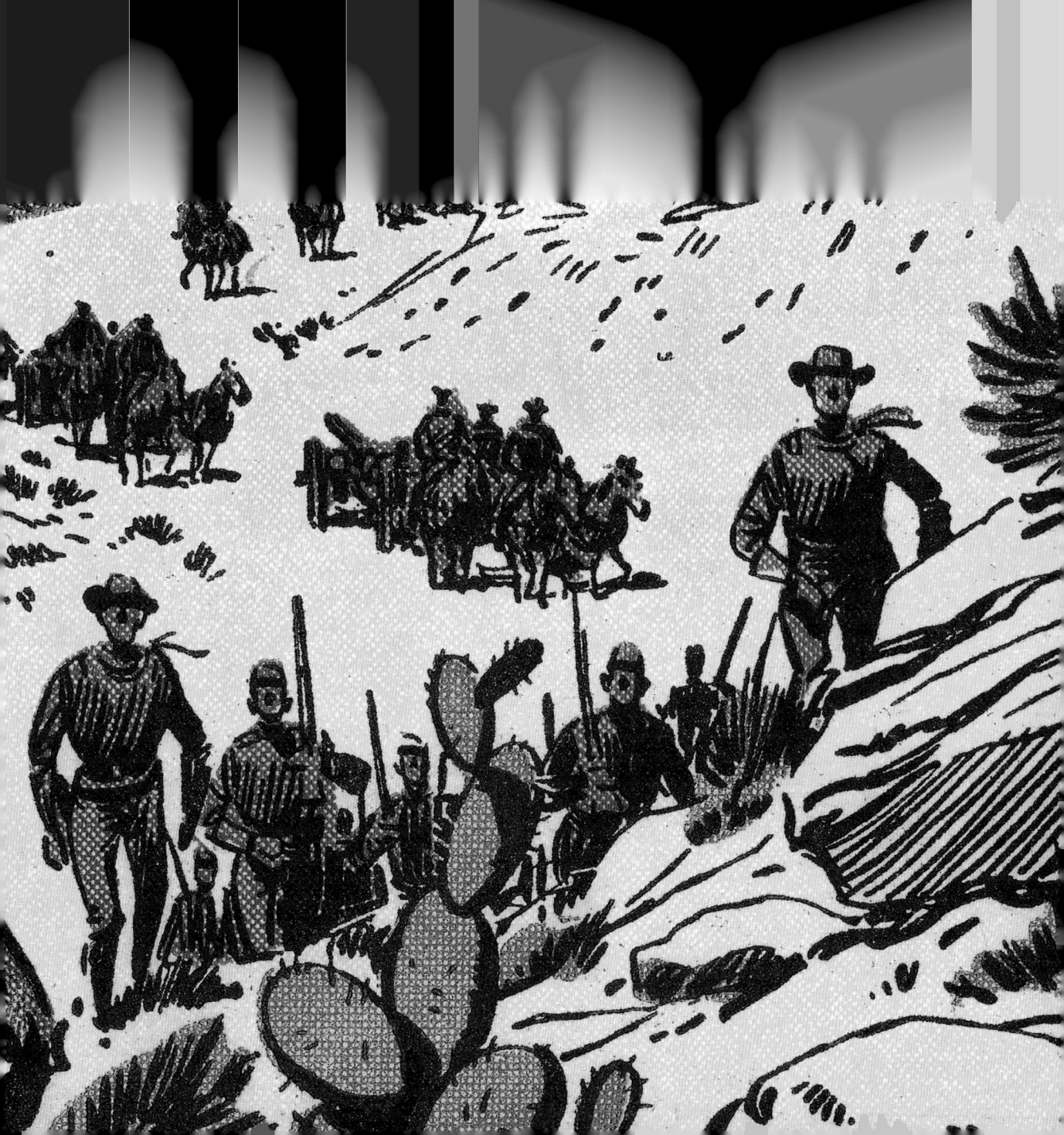

*A*s in most societies where cash and ingredients were in short supply, bread played an important role in the cowboys' diet. Yeasted bread, with its need for true oven baking, was difficult to make on the trail. However, sourdough breads were useful, as were skillet and spoon breads, and biscuits—little quick breads that would cook nicely in a Dutch oven or directly on the fire. Like the cowboys' coffee, biscuits and breads were a significant part of most meals. Almost every cook worth his salt had his own biscuit recipe, which he would guard jealously. Served with a tasty redeye gravy, that is, with added ham or bacon, these biscuits could make a meal in themselves.

Cowboys craved sweet things, and the cook that could provide them regularly was a very popular man. Sugar and dried fruit, particularly apples and apricots, were among the most prized supplies loaded onto the chuck wagon before it set off. There were also lots of wild berries, like the huckleberry, chokecherry, and buffaloberry, which could be found growing along the way, and these were often incorporated into pies and cobblers. The cook often made individual pies for each cowboy, rather than one large pie, and these pies were usually fried instead of baked.

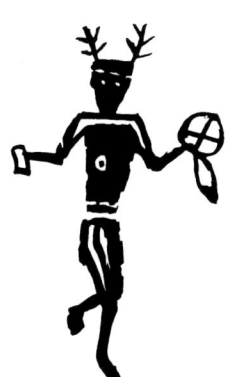

INDIAN FLAT BREADS

Serves 6

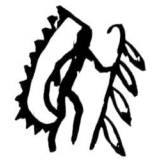

14 oz./1¾ cup (400 g) flour   2 tbsp. powdered milk
2 tbsp. baking powder   1¼ cup (300 ml) warm water
large pinch of salt   vegetable oil, for frying

1 Sift the flour, baking powder, salt, and powdered milk into a large mixing bowl. Add about three-quarters of the warm water and mix in well. Continue adding the warm water a little at a time just until the mixture forms a soft dough that is not sticky. Cover and let rest for about 30 minutes.

2 Divide the dough into 6 portions, roll into balls, and then flatten these into rounds about ¼-in. (5-mm) thick.

3 Heat about ¼ inch oil in a frying pan until quite hot and then cook the rounds one at a time until golden brown on both sides. Drain briefly on crumpled paper towels. Serve while still nice and hot.

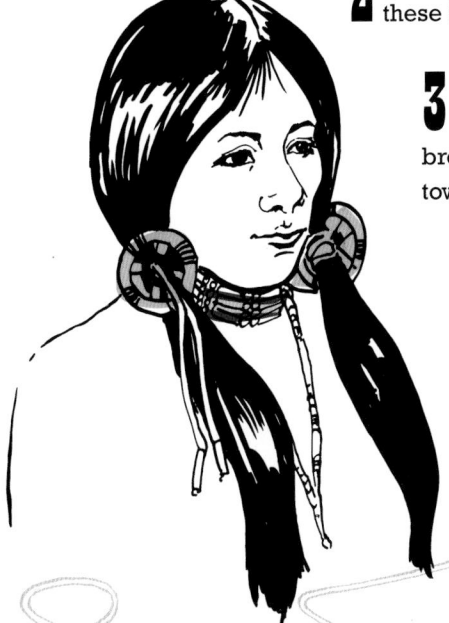

Punchin' Dough

Come, all you young waddies, I'll sing you a song
Stand back from the wagon, stay where you belong
I've heard you observin' I'm fussy and slow,
While you're punchin' the cattle and I'm punchin' dough.

Now I reckon your stomach would grow to your back
If it wa'n't for the cook that keeps fillin' the slack
With the beans in the box and the pork in the tub
I'm a-wonderin' now, who would fill you with grub?

You think you're right handy with gun and with rope
But I've noticed you're bashful when usin' the soap
When you're rollin' your Bull for your brown cigarette
I been rollin' the dough for them biscuits you et.

When you're cuttin' stock, then I'm cuttin' a steak,
When you're wranglin' hosses, I'm wranglin' a cake.
When you're hazin' the dogies and battin' your eyes,
I'm hazin' dried apples that aim to be pies.

You brag about shootin' up windows and lights,
But try shootin' biscuits for twelve appetites;
When you crawl from your roll and the ground it is froze,
Then who biles the coffee that thaws out your nose?

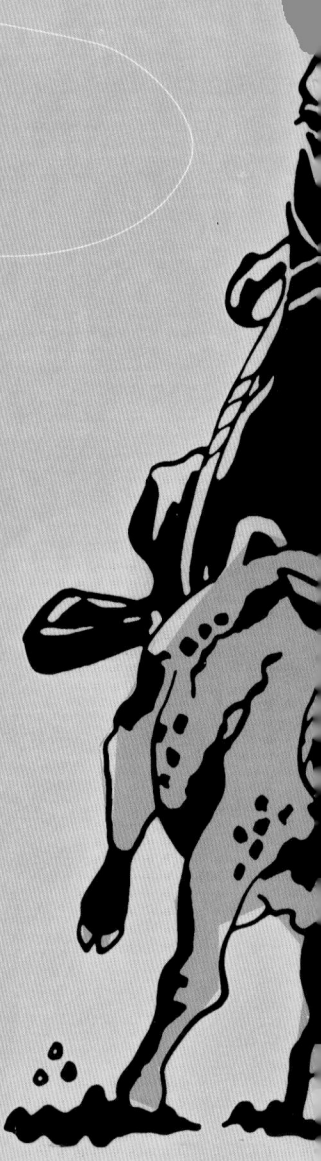

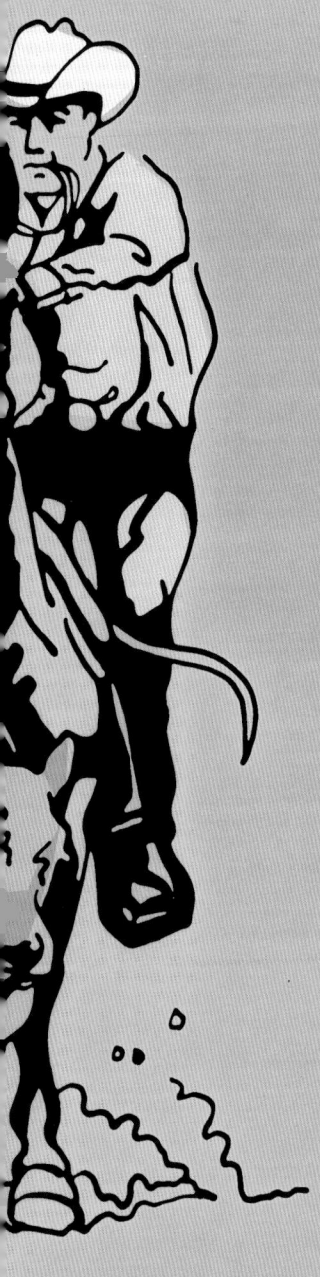

In the old days the punchers took just what they got
It was sow-belly, beans, and the old coffee pot;
But now you come howlin' for pie and for cake,
Then you cuss at the cook for a good bellyache.

You say that I'm old, with my feet on the skids
Well, I'm tellin' you now that you're nothin' but kids
If you reckon your mounts are some snaky and raw,
Just try ridin herd on a stove that won't draw.

When you look at my apron, you're readin' my brand
Four-X, which is sign for the best in the land
On bottie or sack it sure stands for good luck,
So line up, you waddies, and wrangle your chuck.

No use to your snortin' and fightin' your head
If you like it with chili, just eat what I said:
For I aim to be boss of this end of the show
While you're punchin' cattle and I'm punchin' dough.

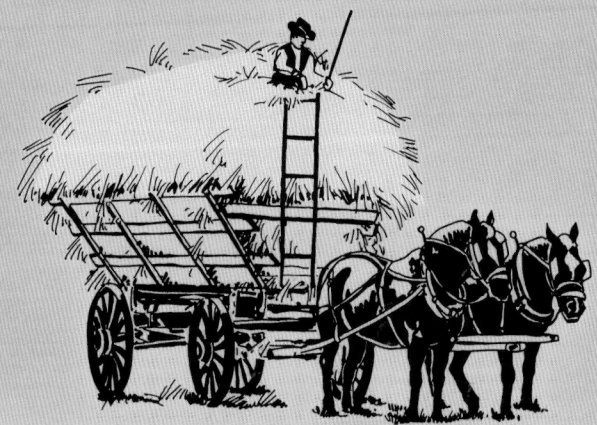

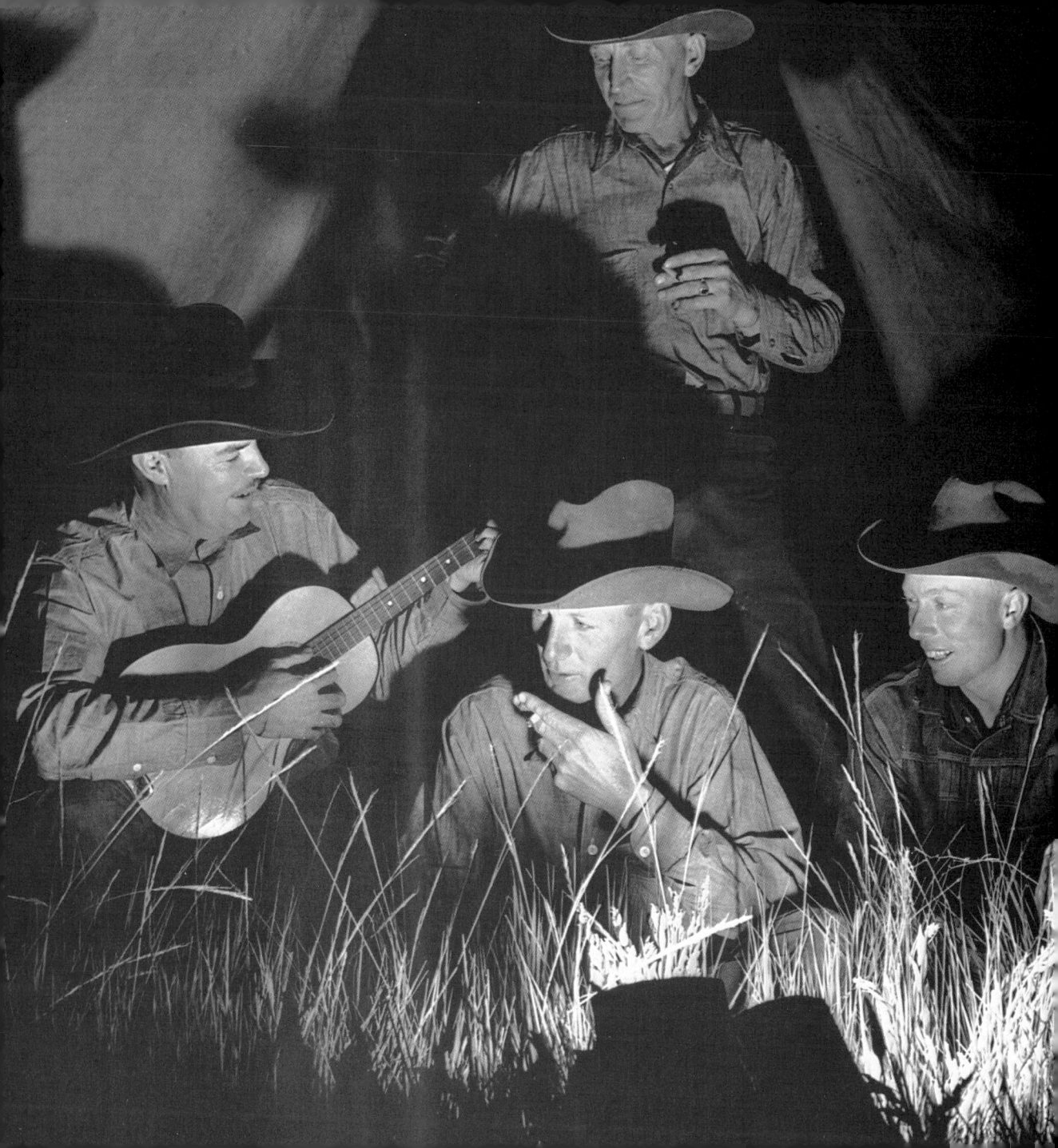

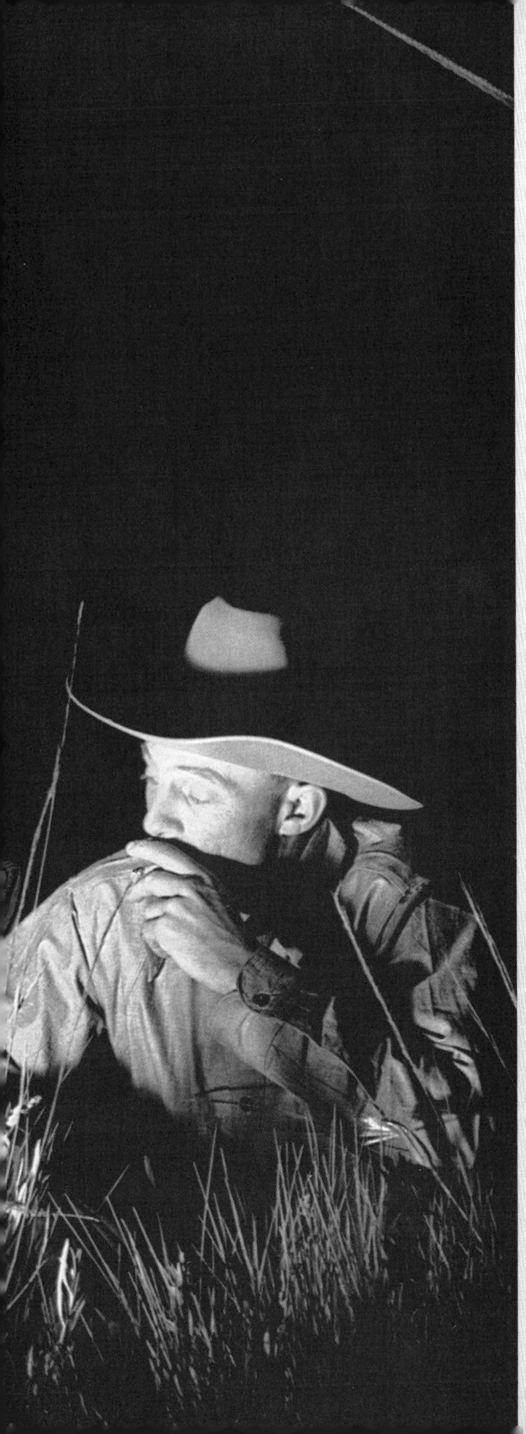

*"AS I WAS A-WALKING ONE MORNING
    FOR PLEASURE
I SPIED A COWPUNCHER A-RIDING ALONG,
HIS HAT WAS THROWED BACK AND HIS
    SPURS WAS A-JINGLING,
AS HE APPROACH'D ME A-SINGING THIS
    SONG."*

Author unknown
FROM GIT ALONG LITTLE DOGIES

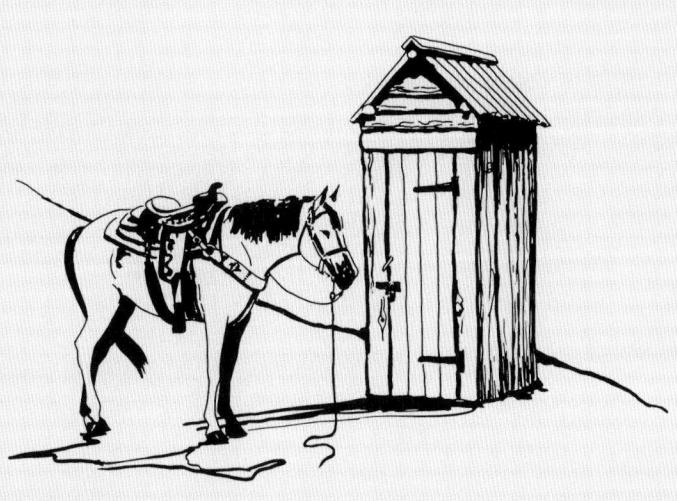

SKILLET CORN BREAD

Serves 6

4 oz./½ cup (85 g) cornmeal
or quick-cooking polenta
4 oz./½ cup (85 g) flour
1 tbsp. baking powder
½ tsp. salt

2 large eggs
12 fl. oz./1½ cups (350 ml) milk
4 tbsp. vegetable oil
3 oz. (85 g) cooked corn kernels

1 In a large bowl, combine the cornmeal or polenta, flour, baking powder, and salt.

2 In a small bowl, beat the egg, then beat in the milk and oil. Pour this into the flour mixture and stir until blended. Stir in the corn kernels.

3 Lightly oil a deep frying pan, get it quite hot, and pour in the mixture. Cover tightly. (If your pan doesn't have a lid, cover with foil as tightly as you can. Over that, place a lid from another pan to hold the foil in place.) Cook over a moderate heat for 20 to 25 minutes.

Your can flavor this bread in all sorts of ways: Add chopped onions and/or chilies or chili flakes, and/or cooked bacon or shredded cheese to the mixture, or just sprinkle on some shredded cheese before covering.

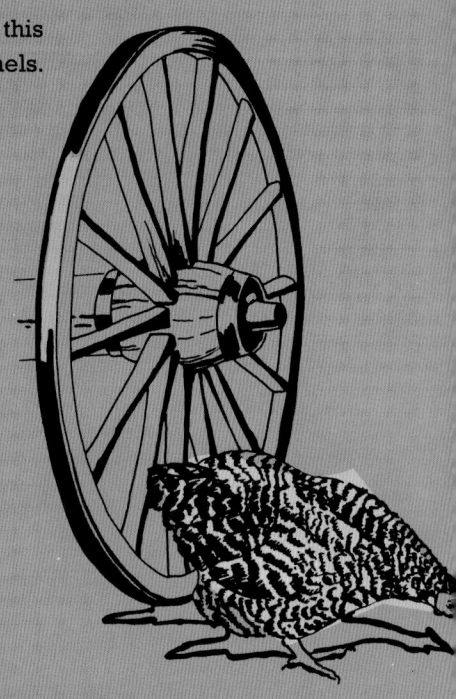

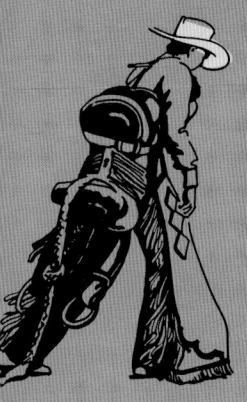

SPOON BREAD

Serves 4

2 oz./¼ cup (45 g) flour	or quick-cooking polenta
1 tsp. salt	1 egg, beaten
1 tsp. baking powder	12 fl. oz./1½ cups (350 ml) milk
1 tsp. sugar	1 oz. (25 g) butter
6 oz./¾ cup (125 g) cornmeal	

1 Sift the flour, salt, and baking powder into a mixing bowl. Add the sugar and cornmeal or polenta, and mix well.

2 Add the beaten egg and two-thirds of the milk. Mix to a smooth batter.

3 Melt the butter in a heavy-duty pot that has a tight-fitting lid. When the butter is good and hot, pour in the batter. Pour the remaining milk over it, cover tightly, and cook over a moderate heat for about 30 minutes, until the spoon bread is nice and crusty on the bottom and cooked through.

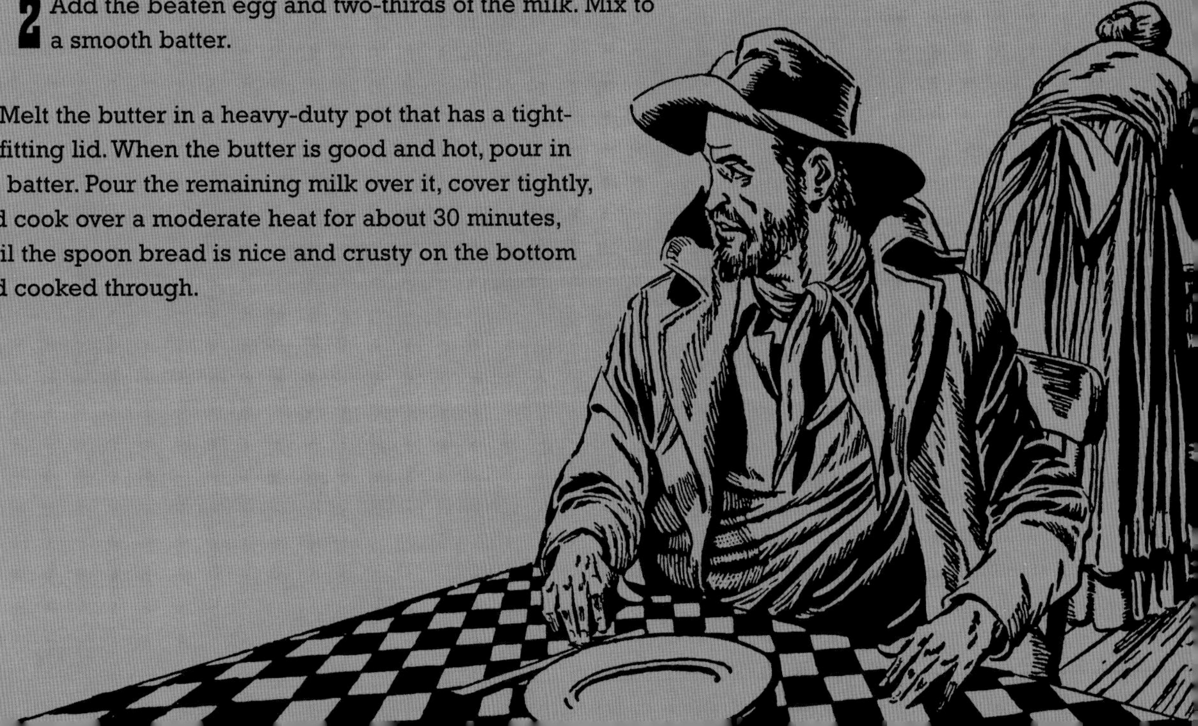

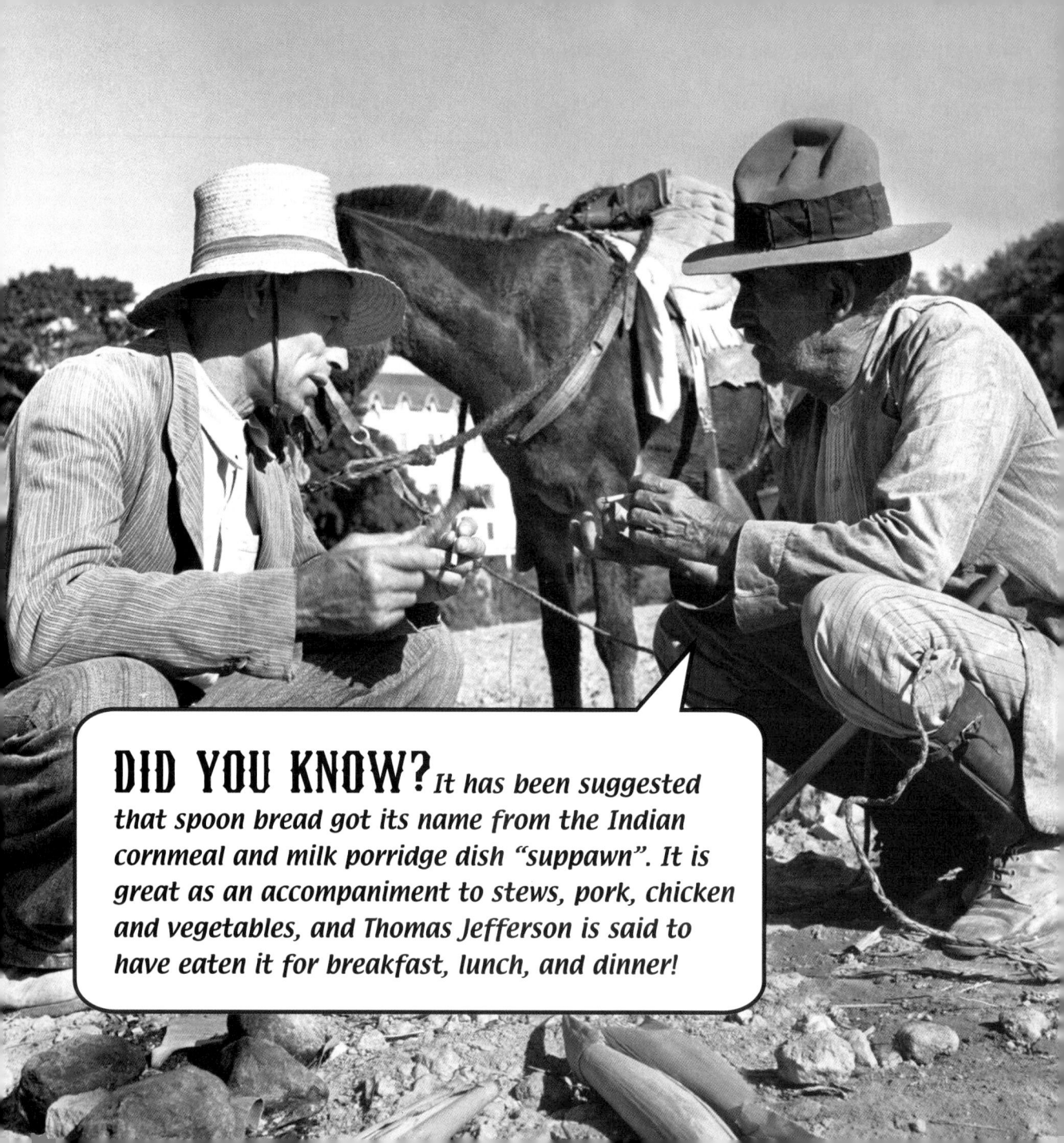

DID YOU KNOW? *It has been suggested that spoon bread got its name from the Indian cornmeal and milk porridge dish "suppawn". It is great as an accompaniment to stews, pork, chicken and vegetables, and Thomas Jefferson is said to have eaten it for breakfast, lunch, and dinner!*

Twisted Willow Campfire Bread

Serves 4

12 oz./1½ cups (350 g) flour
pinch of salt
¼ tsp. baking soda

1 oz./2 tbsp. (25 g) butter, diced small

1 Trim 4 willow (or other suitable) branches into long sticks for cooking the bread over a fire or barbecue. Scrub them well and then soak them in water for at least half an hour so they won't char.

2 Sift the four, salt, and baking soda into a bowl. Add the butter and cut in until the flour mixture resembles crumbs. Mix in just enough cold water to make a stiff dough, then set aside to rest for a few minutes.

3 Cut the rested dough into 4 pieces and then twist each piece around the top of a prepared willow stick. Cook over the fire or barbecue, turning from time to time to ensure even cooking, until golden brown all over.

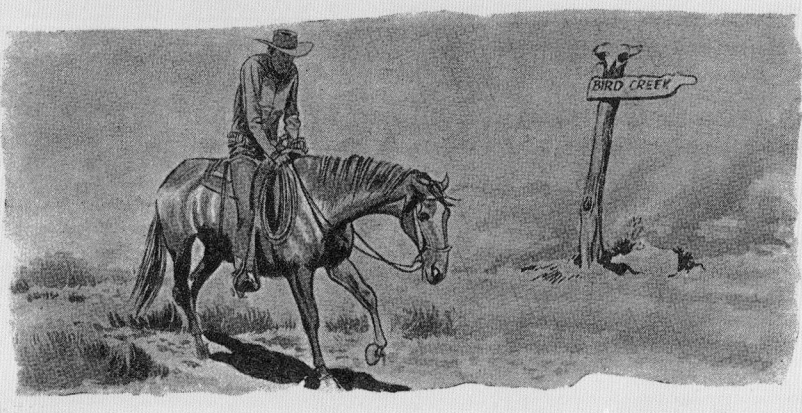

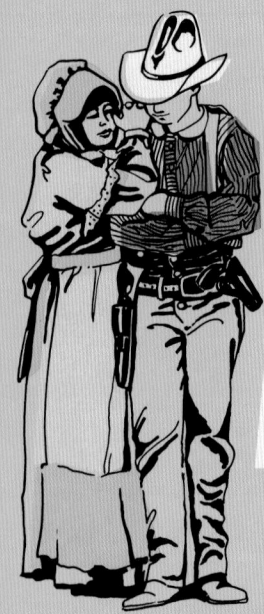

FRIED APPLE PIES

Makes 8-10

8 oz. (225 g) dried apples
the juice of ½ lemon
6-8 oz./¾-1 cup (175–225 g) sugar
1 tsp. ground cinnamon
1 tsp. ground allspice
pinch of salt
1 tbsp. cornstarch
vegetable oil, for frying

For the pastry:
8 oz./1 cup (225 g) flour
pinch of salt
4 oz./8 tbsp. (115 g) chilled butter,
cut into small pieces
1 small egg

1 The day before: Put the apples in a pan, barely cover with hot water, stir in the lemon juice, and leave overnight.

2 The next day, bring the pan to a boil, lower the heat, and simmer for about 20 minutes, stirring occasionally and mashing some of the apples to a purée, until the apples are tender. Mix in sugar to taste (depending on the sweetness of the apples), along with the cinnamon, allspice, and salt. Add a little liquid and just enough cornstarch to make a paste and stir into the apple mixture. Cook until the liquid is a saucelike consistency. Simmer for a few minutes. Let cool.

3 Make the pastry: Sift the flour and salt into a mixing bowl. Add the diced butter and cut it in until the mixture resembles coarse crumbs. Beat the egg in a large measuring cup and add enough cold water to make it up to 3 fl. oz./⅓ cup (85 ml). Make a well in the flour and pour the egg mixture into it. Stir the flour slowly into the liquid until it comes together as a dough. Gather up into a ball, cover with plastic wrap, and chill for at least 30 minutes.

4 Divide the dough into 8 to 10 pieces. Roll into balls and flatten into rounds about 5 in. (12.5 cm). Spoon the apple mixture on one side of each round, leaving a 1-in. (2.5-cm) clear border. Moisten the edges with water, fold over, and press and pinch the edges to make a well-sealed turnover. If you like, decorate the edges by pressing with a fork. Chill briefly.

5 Pour about ¼ in. oil into a large frying pan and heat until a piece of dry bread browns in 60 seconds. Fry the pies in batches, for 2 minutes on each side, until golden brown. Drain briefly on crumpled paper towels. Serve nice and hot.

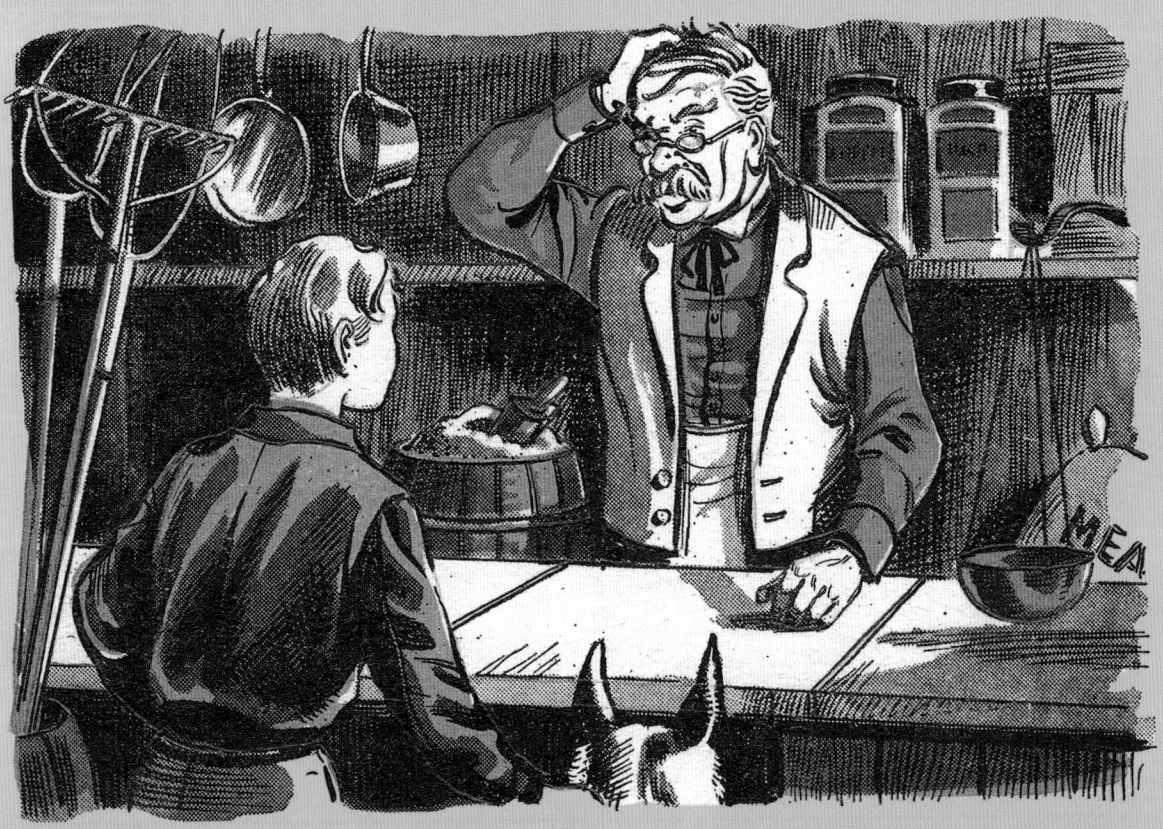

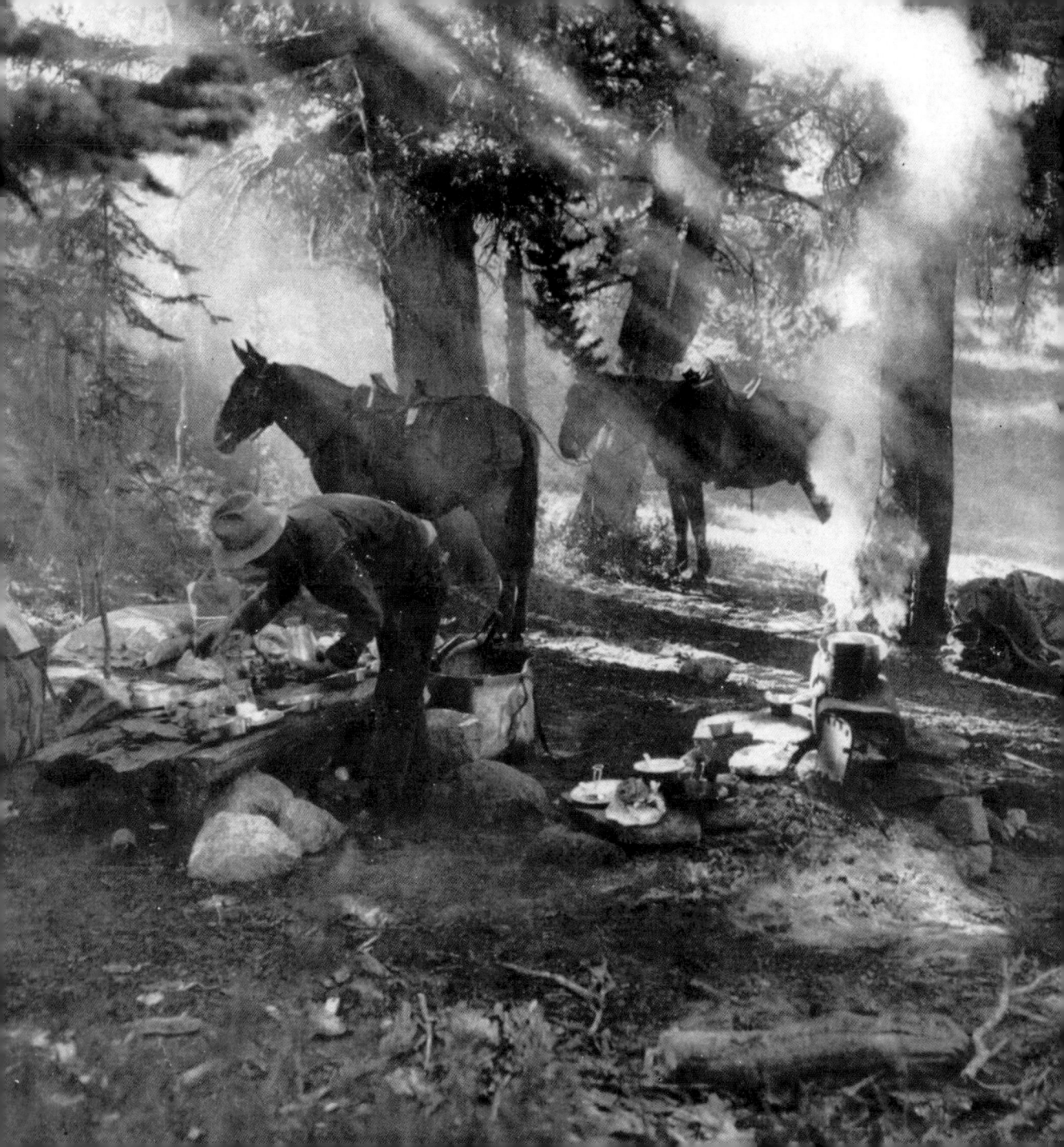

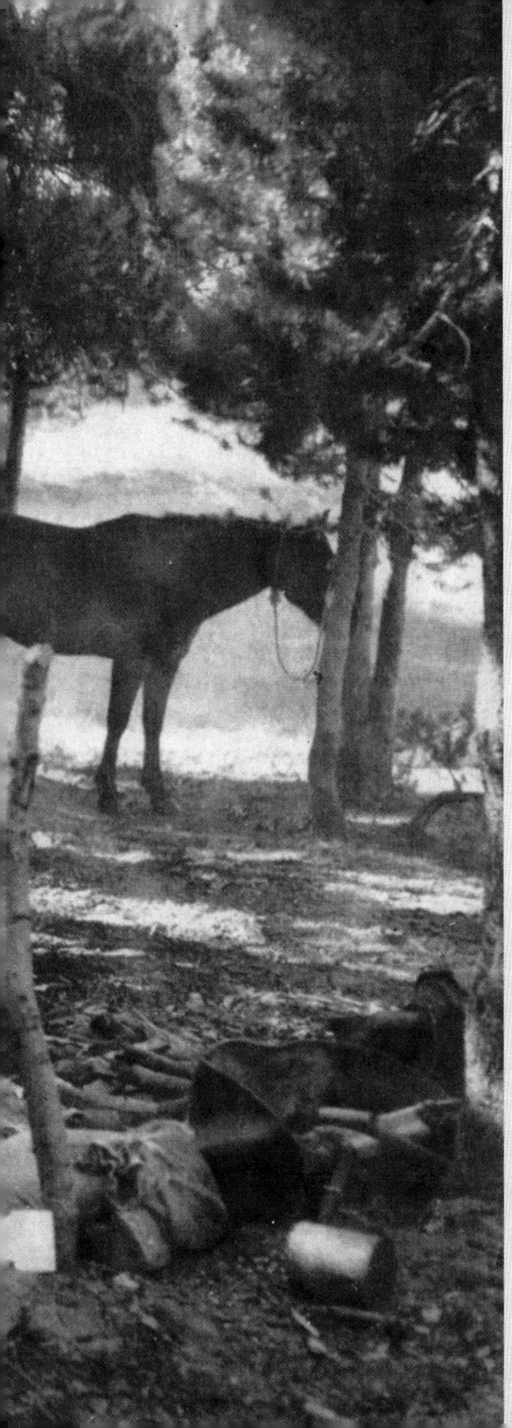

*"WE CAMP, AND GO, AND CARE NO JOT
HOW SOON, HOW FAR WE ROAM...
BUT EACH CAMP-FIRE HAS MARKED A SPOT
THAT MEN SHALL CALL THEIR HOME."*

Arthur W. Jose
FROM THE PIONEERS

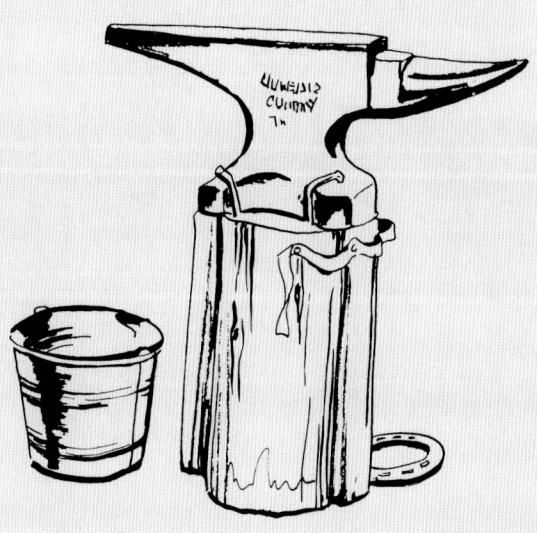

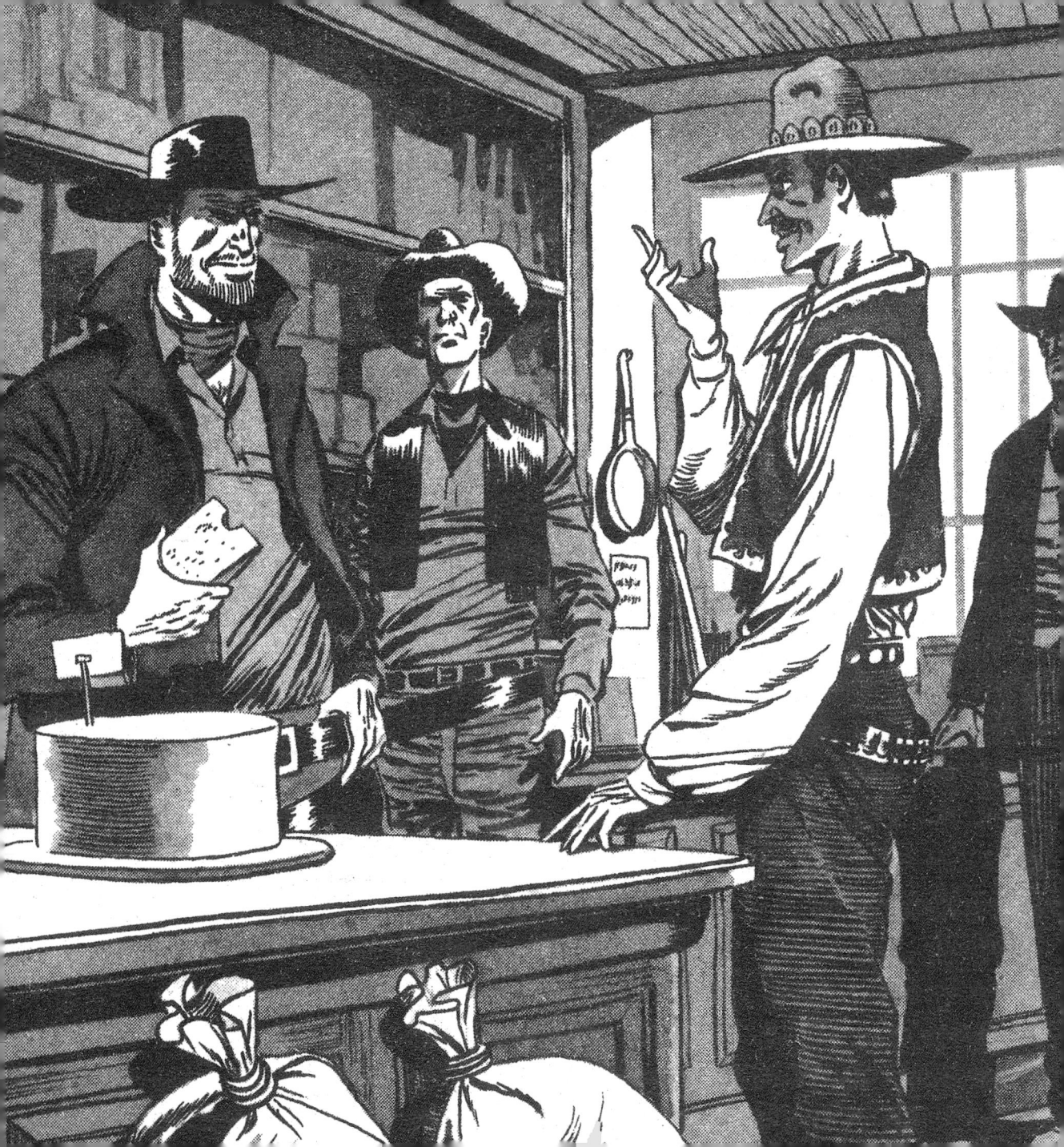

CANNONBALL PUDDING

8 oz./1 cup (225 g) flour
2 slices of fresh bread, grated
into breadcrumbs
3 oz./⅓ cup (85 g) brown sugar
2 tsp. baking soda
1 tsp. salt
2 tsp. ground cinnamon
large pinch of ground ginger
large pinch of freshly
grated nutmeg

large pinch of ground cloves
6 oz./¾ cup (175 g) seedless raisins
4 oz./½ cup (115 g) minced suet
2 oz./¼ cup (50 g) chopped pecans
or walnuts
4 fl. oz./½ cup (125 ml) evaporated milk
2 eggs, beaten
4 fl. oz./½ cup (125 ml) light molasses
3–4 good spoonfuls of whiskey (optional)
cream, to serve (optional)

1 In a large mixing bowl, combine the flour, breadcrumbs, sugar, baking soda, salt, and spices. Fold in the dried fruit, suet, and nuts. Stir in the evaporated milk, eggs, molasses, and whiskey if using it.

2 Line a large heatproof bowl or colander with a large clean tea towel or foil (cowboys would make this pudding larger and cook it in a sack) and spoon the mixture into it. Bring up the sides of the cloth or foil and tie together, leaving lots of room for expansion. Set the bowl in a large pan with a tight-fitting lid, add boiling water to come halfway up the sides of the bowl, cover, and place over heat so that it bubbles gently. Leave to steam for about 2 hours, adding water when and if necessary.

3 Remove from the pan, unwrap, and let sit for about 20 minutes before serving. If you are lucky enough to have some cream, pour that over the pudding to serve.

You can make this lighter by adding three more eggs: Separate them, and stir in the yolks with the suet. Beat the whites to a good froth, and fold into the final mixture. You can also add more dried fruit if you like, such as apples. If using liquor, sprinkle some more over the resting cooked pudding for a real kick, or stir some into the cream.

When I lay down at night by a camp fire's light
And the work of the day is done
Then I wouldn't exchange my home on the range
For anything under the sun.
There's peace and rest out here in the west
Not found in your cities so grand
And when cowboys sing, the prairies ring
With music that I understand.

by Carson Robison

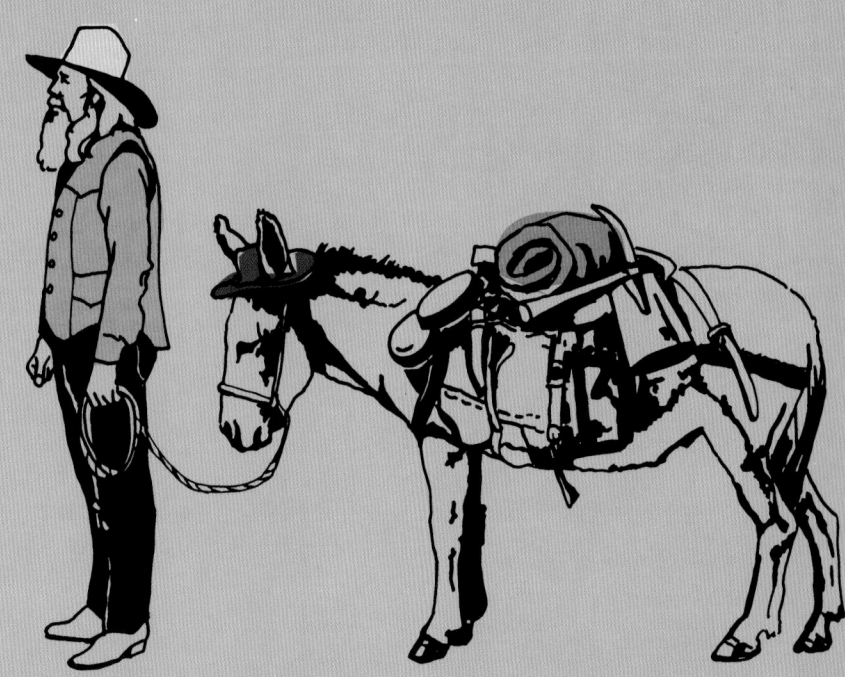

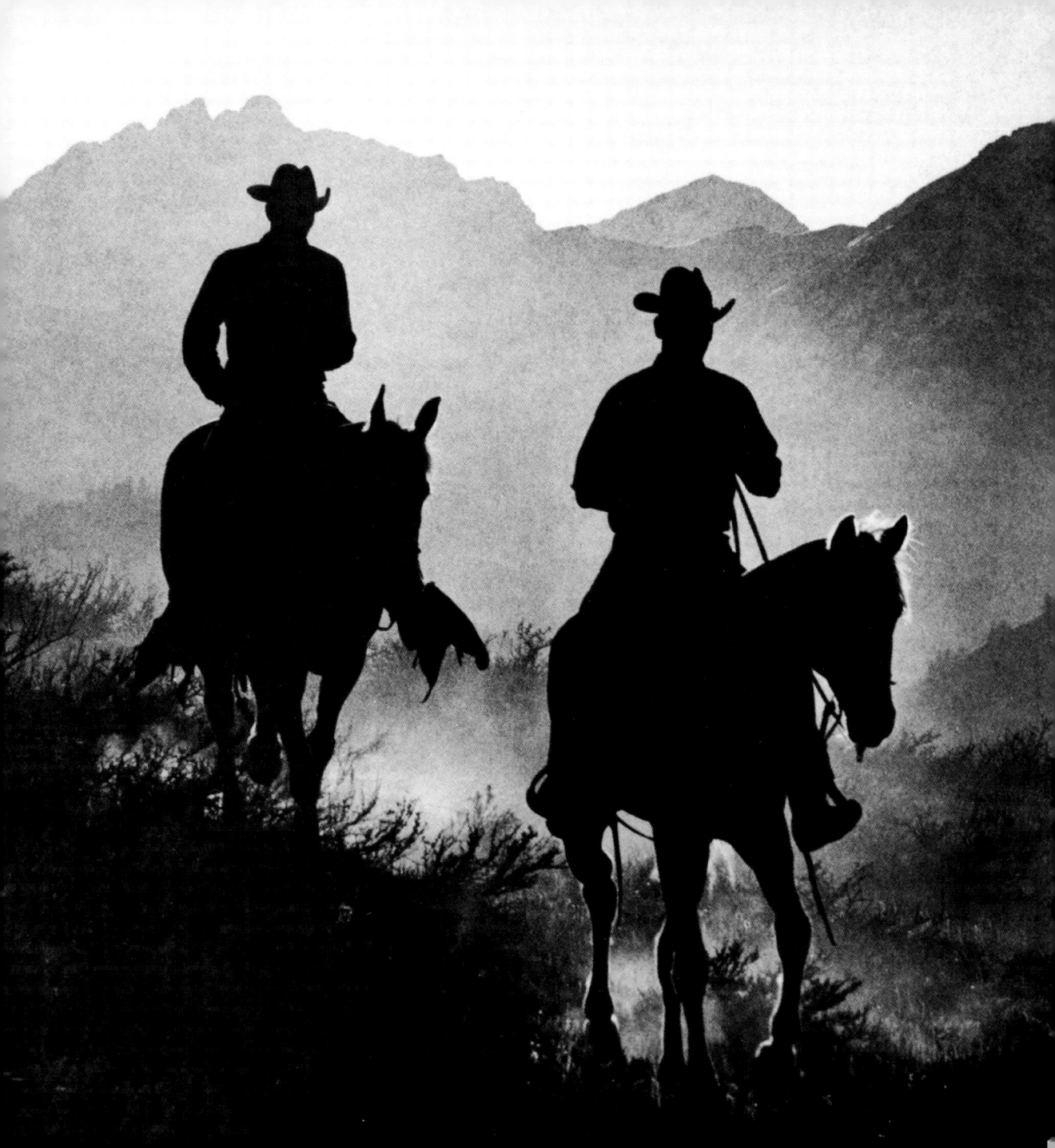

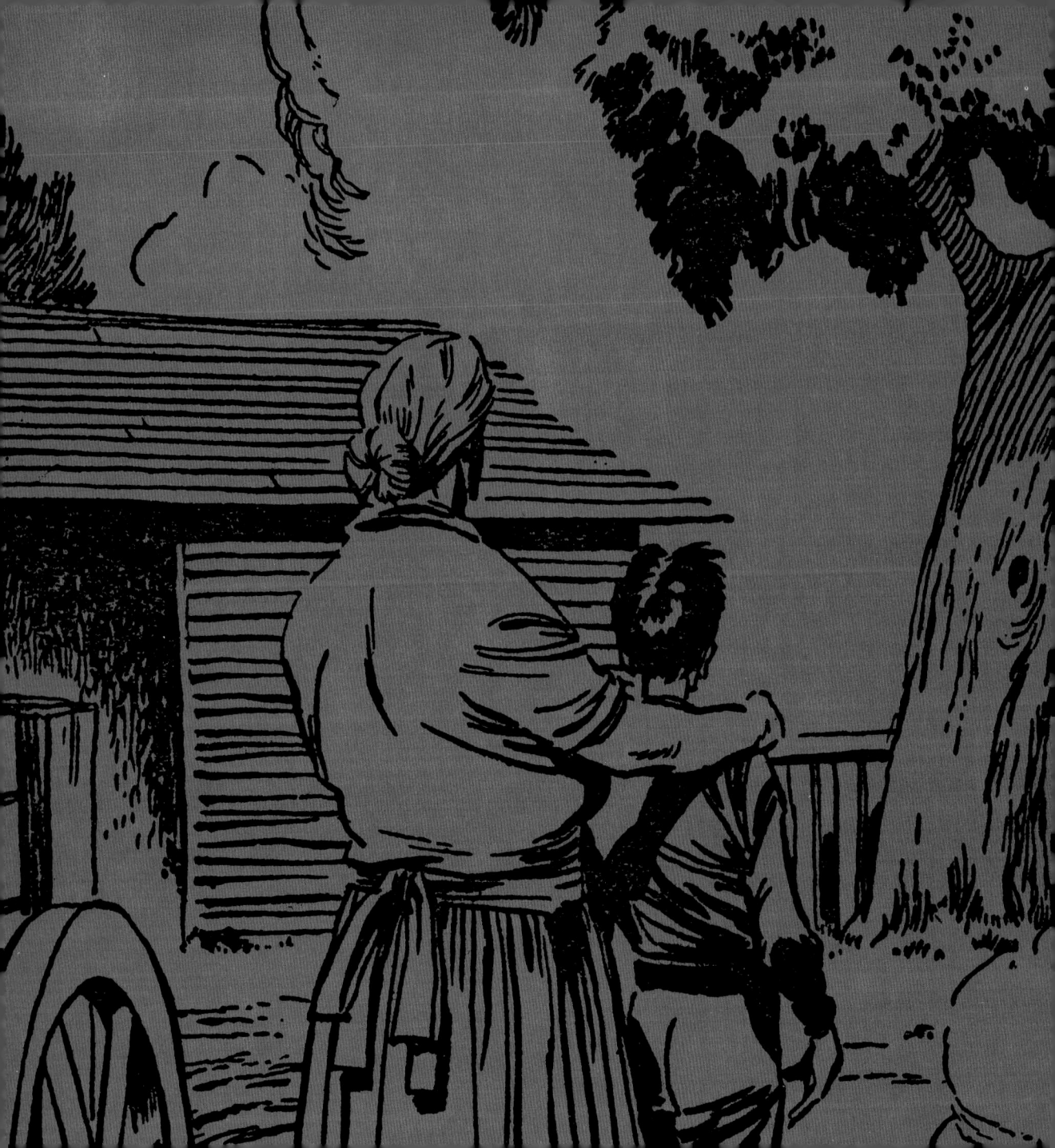

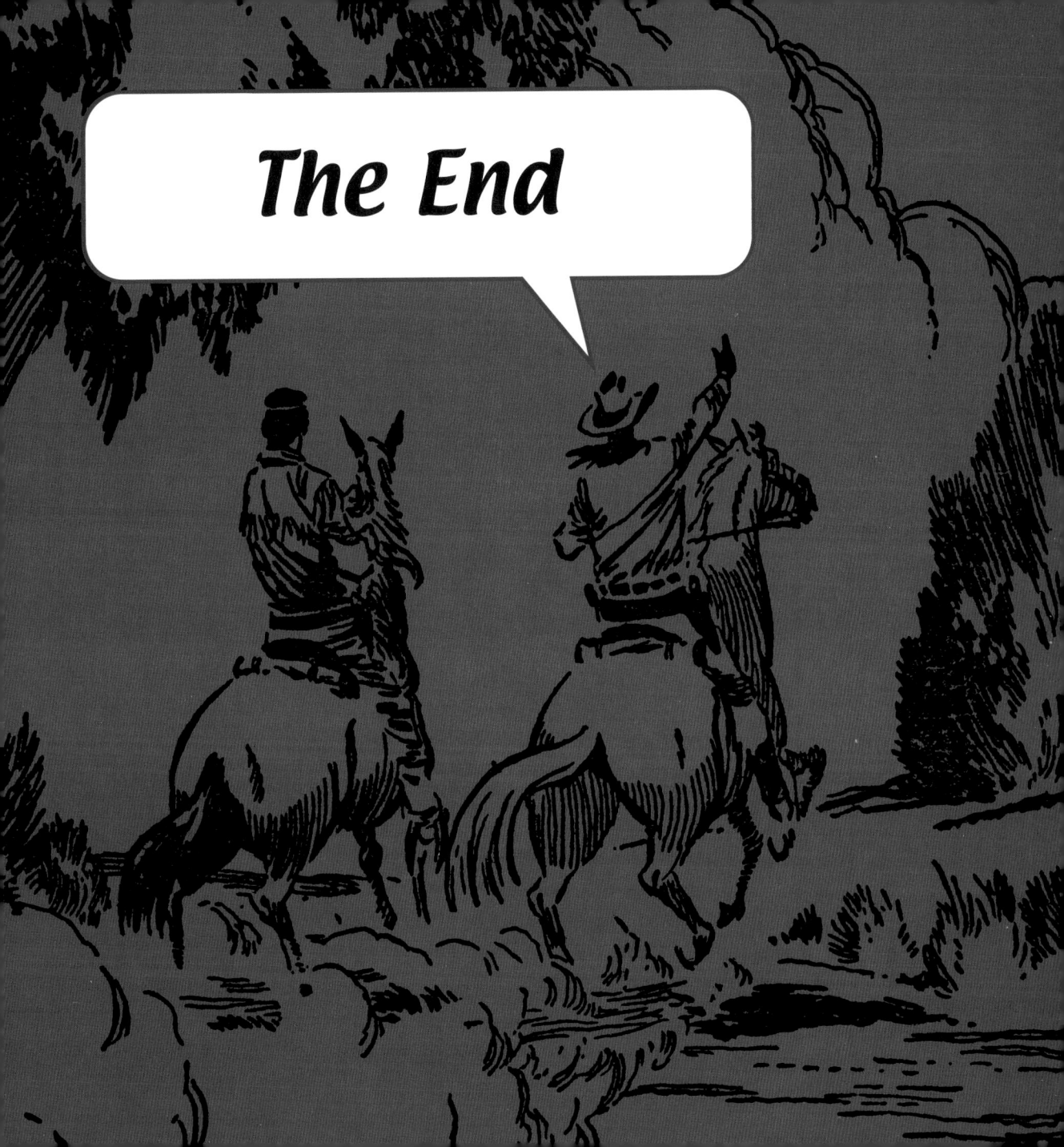

PICTURE CREDITS

cover: Cowboy camp, 1965, © Joe Monroe/Getty Images.

p.10: Ranchers eat by the chuck wagon, 1919, © CORBIS.

p.20: Elderly gold prospector with burro, © Bettman/CORBIS.

p.29: Cowboys stopping for coffee break, © Bettman/CORBIS.

p.32: A Gaucho Roping a Steer, circa 1930–1970, © Hulton–Deutsch Collection/CORBIS.

p.36: Cowboys herding cattle on horseback, circa 1940, © Horace Bristol/CORBIS.

p.45: Four cowboys survey the range, 1952, © Hulton–Deutsch Collection/CORBIS.

p.52: Cowboys eating beside chuck wagon, 1905, © CORBIS.

p.57: Farmers shucking corn, 1941, © CORBIS.

p.58: Cattle ranchers lined up for lunch, circa 1940, © Horace Bristol/CORBIS.

p.61: Cowboy seated Indian style eating, 1927, © Bettman/CORBIS.

p.64: Cowboys around the chuck wagon, circa 1890, © Bettman/CORBIS.

p.72: Cowboy on cattle drive, circa 1970–1985, © Buddy Mays/CORBIS.

p.78: Shopkeepers & customers before stores, 1894, © Bettman/CORBIS.

p.84: Map of Texas & cowboys roping cattle, © Bettmann/CORBIS.

p.87: Lyndon B. Johnson eating spareribs, 1964, © Bettmann/CORBIS.

p.98: Teddy Roosevelt on horseback, © Underwood & Underwood/CORBIS.

p.103: Cover of Beadle's Dime New York Library, circa 1955, © Bettmann/CORBIS.

p.110: Cowboys singing at the campfire, 1939, © CORBIS.

p.114: Squatting cowboys swapping stories, 1942, © Genevieve Naylor/CORBIS.

p.123: Cowboys looking for stray cattle, 1959, © Josef Scaylea/CORBIS.

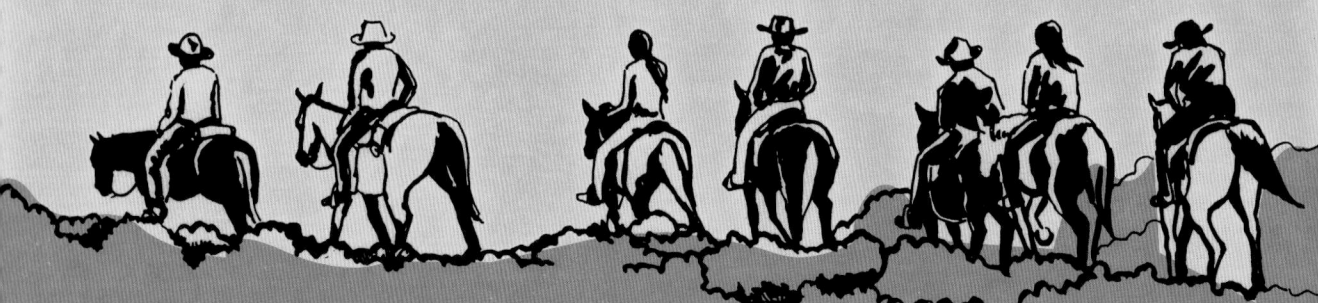

TEXT CREDITS

p. 11: Reprinted with the permission of Scribner, an imprint of Simon & Schuster Adult Publishing Group, from THE AMERICAN WEST by Dee Brown. Copyright © 1995 by Dee Brown and the Estate of Martin F. Schmitt.

pp. 18–19: *Mornin' Business* by Lee Henry, email: bellyup@benjacklarado.com

p. 21: extract from STUDY OUT THE LAND by T. K. Whipple (Ayer Company Publishers, 1943).

pp. 28–29: extract from *Cowboy Coffee* by Rod Miller, from COWBOYS ARE PART HUMAN: A COLLECTION OF WESTERN POETRY, edited by Ellen Schmidt and Dana Schreur (Southwest Whispers, 1998).

p. 50: Reprinted with permission of Simon & Schuster Adult Publishing Group, from THE COWBOY LIFE by Michele Morris. Copyright © 1993 by Michele Morris.

p. 56: extract from BENJAMIN FRANKLIN BOOK OF RECIPES by Hilaire Dubourq (Canopus Publishing, 2000).

p. 60: extract from WE POINTED THEM NORTH: RECOLLECTIONS OF A COWPUNCHER, E. C. Abbott and Helen H. Smith. Reprinted by Permission of the University of Oklahoma Press, Norman.

p. 76: quote from Teddy Blue Abbott, 1879, from THE WEST: AN ILLUSTRATED HISTORY by Geoffrey Ward (Little, Brown & Co., 1996).

p. 122: poem from THE NEWEST CARSON ROBISON COLLECTION OF 23 SONGS, AND JUST A POEM OR TWO by Carson Robison (Robbins Music Corporation and Francis, Day & Hunter Ltd, 1930s) © Carson J. Robison.

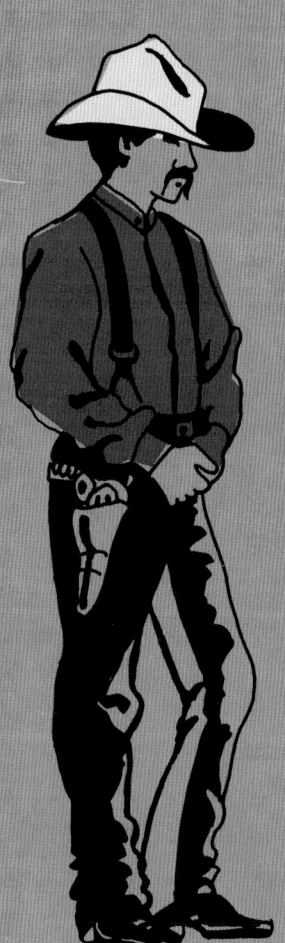

Note: Every effort has been made to contact current copyright holders. Any omission is unintentional and the publisher would be pleased to hear from any copyright holders not acknowledged above.

Index